Taking
Responsibility
for the Past

Taking Responsibility for the Past

Reparation and Historical Injustice

Janna Thompson

polity

First published in 2002 by Polity Press in association with Blackwell Publishers Ltd, a Blackwell Publishing Company.

Editorial office:
Polity Press
65 Bridge Street
Cambridge CB2 1UR, UK

Marketing and production:
Blackwell Publishers Ltd
108 Cowley Road
Oxford OX4 1JF, UK

Published in the USA by
Blackwell Publishers Inc.
350 Main Street
Malden, MA 02148, USA

A catalogue record for this book is available from the British Library.

Library of Congress Cataloging-in-Publication Data

Thompson, Janna, 1942-
   Taking responsibility for the past : reparation and historical injustice / Janna Thompson.
      p. cm.
Includes bibliographical references and index.
   ISBN 0–7456–2884–2 (hb : alk. paper) — ISBN 0–7456–2885–0 (pbk.)
   1. Reparations. 2. Intergenerational relations. 3. Restorative justice. I. Title
KZ6785 .T49 2002
   323.1′1—dc21   2002003638

Typeset in 10.5 on 12 pt Sabon by Kolam Information Services Pvt. Ltd., Pondicherry, India

This book is printed on acid-free paper.

Contents

Acknowledgements

My work on this project was supported by a grant from the Australian Research Council and by a fellowship from the Centre for Applied Philosophy and Public Ethics at Melbourne University. A large number of individuals have provided valuable critical responses and advice at various stages or helped me in other ways. I wish to give special thanks to Judith Baker, John Campbell, Robert Fox, Robert Fullinwider, Will Kymlicka, Hugh LaFollette, Bruce Langtry, David Lyons, Lukas Meyer, Alexandre Pavkovic, Ross Poole, Igor Primoratz, Michael Ridge, Christine Sypnowich, Robert Young, and to my research assistants Penelope Davies and Glynis Jones.

The approach I take to transgenerational obligations was first developed in 'Inherited obligation and the value of community', *Canadian Journal of Philosophy*, 29(4) (1999), 493–516. In writing chapters 1 and 2 I made use of material first published in 'Historical obligations', *Australasian Journal of Philosophy*, 78 (2000), 334–45. Chapters 7–9 are based on material first published in 'Historical injustice and reparation: justifying claims of descendants', *Ethics*, 112 (2001), 114–35.

In chapter 9 I also drew on material from 'Injustice and the removal of Aboriginal children', *Australian Journal of Professional and Applied Ethics*, 2 (2000), 2–13. I also owe thanks to the editors and referees of these journals.

Janna Thompson
Philosophy, La Trobe University
Centre for Applied Philosophy and Public Ethics,
Melbourne University

Introduction: History and Responsibility

History is a tale of unrequited injustice. Treaties have been broken, communities wiped out, cultures plundered or destroyed, innocent people betrayed, slaughtered, enslaved, robbed, and exploited, and no recompense has ever been made to victims or their descendants. Historical injustices cast a long shadow. Their effects can linger long after the perpetrators and their victims are dead. They haunt the memories of descendants, blight the history of peoples, and poison relations between communities. They are the root cause of many existing inequities. Historical grievances have provided people with a justification for enmity, a reason for seeking revenge. They are at the heart of some of the bloodiest struggles and deeds in both historical and contemporary times. For many of the descendants and successors of those who were wronged, they are a motivation for seeking justice – the focus of demands for reparation.

Demands for reparation for historical injustices have come to public attention in recent years, particularly in those places where law or public opinion makes it more likely that they will be taken seriously. Native Americans and Canadians have fought, and sometimes won, court cases for the restoration of ancient treaty rights or lands lost through unjust dispossession. Australian Aborigines, whose demands for land rights were long ignored, have obtained a legal basis for claiming rights over some of the land that was taken from them in the course of European settlement. New Zealand Maoris demanded, and had restored to them, some of the rights guaranteed to their communities by the Treaty of Waitangi signed by their ancestors in 1840. Reparations are still being paid by German governments to survivors of Nazi atrocities or their heirs, and some German companies have agreed to pay compensation to those who were forced to work as slaves in their factories. American and Canadian Japanese who were interned during World War II have won token recompense from their governments for their ordeal. Eastern European governments have adopted policies allowing people dispossessed by Communist regimes, or their heirs, to make claims for return of property.

In the 1960s James Forman, a black activist, received much publicity, some sympathy and also criticism for his demand that churches and synagogues pay $500 million in reparations for the historical role their organizations played in the exploitation of American blacks.[1] Demands for black reparations have been revived by the success of American Japanese in having their historical grievances addressed.

> The United States has finally apologized to its Japanese Americans for the racially based horrors visited upon them for four years and awarded them financial compensation. May we hope that this consciousness raising exercise has helped sensitize the body politic to addressing the far greater injustices inflicted on Africans and their descendants on this continent over more than three centuries.[2]

Demands for reparation for slavery are not confined to African Americans. That Africans should be compensated for harm resulting from the transatlantic slave trade was proposed by African states and organizations as a topic for discussion at the recent World Conference Against Racism.[3]

Heads of governments, officials, churches and corporations have become increasingly willing to acknowledge past injustices committed by their communities or organizations. An epidemic of apology has swept the globe. Former American President Clinton apologized for the US violation of Hawaiian sovereignty in 1893, British Prime Minister Blair for British policy during the Irish potato famine. The Canadian Government apologized to indigenous communities for policies aimed at destroying their culture. Pope John Paul II asked forgiveness for all the sins committed by the Catholic Church in the last 2000 years. Queen Elizabeth apologized for the British exploitation of the Maoris, the Japanese Prime Minister for atrocities committed by Japanese in Korea and China during World War II. Some former government officials in South Africa have acknowledged and apologized for their activities during the period of apartheid.[4] However, leaders have sometimes resisted the pressure to apologize. Clinton judged it not in the national interest to apologize for slavery. John Howard, the present Prime Minister of Australia, persistently refuses to apologize for injustices committed against Aborigines. Present generations, he says, should not be expected to take responsibility for crimes committed in the past. Nevertheless, many Australians, as individuals or members of organizations, have demonstrated that they are prepared to accept this responsibility.[5]

Demands for reparation or apology for historical injustice and the increasing willingness of people to meet these demands are part of what Elazar Barkan identifies as an outbreak of morality in the affairs of nations.

> Beginning at the end of World War II, and quickening since the end of the Cold War, questions of morality and justice are receiving growing attention as political questions. As such, the need for restitution to past victims has become a major part of national politics and international diplomacy.[6]

This development poses some important historical and political questions. However, the focus of this study is on the moral demands themselves. It is premised on a belief that they should be taken seriously – not merely as pressures that politicians have to deal with, but as claims that require a response from us as moral agents. To respond appropriately, we have to attend to what is being demanded and reflect on whether these demands are justified. Moral reflection on responsibilities with respect to the past would be appropriate even if concern about historical injustices was not so widespread or politically influential. The fact that demands based on history have become so prevalent merely makes the inquiry more urgent.

Some definitions

The moral issues raised by demands for reparation show the need for a systematic inquiry into the existence, nature and extent of historical obligations and entitlements. A historical obligation, as I will understand it in this study, is a moral responsibility incurred by individuals as citizens, owners or executives of corporations, or members of some other transgenerational association or community, as the result of the commitments or actions of their predecessors. Past actions are connected to present responsibilities by means of a moral argument. For example: 'We ought to keep the treaties made by our national predecessors because treaties ought to be honoured'; 'We ought to make recompense for the dispossession of indigenous people because this was unjust, and injustices require reparation.' The past is a source of obligation not merely because of the effect of past deeds on present conditions. Historical obligations are duties defined by past happenings – by the fact that a treaty was signed or an unjust deed done.

Historical obligations belong to the more general category of 'past-referring obligations', which include the duty to keep promises and honour contracts, to pay debts and make recompense for wrongs done, to avoid punishing the innocent (and, many people would add, to punish the guilty). Past-referring obligations are historical when those who are supposed to be responsible for keeping the promise, honouring the contract, paying the debt, or making reparation are not the ones who made the promise or did the deeds, but their descendants or successors. In many cases those to whom historical obligations are supposed to be owed are not the victims themselves, but their descendants or successors. These successors are claiming a historical entitlement. A historical injustice, as I will understand it, is a wrong done either to or by past people.

An obligation implies the existence of a corresponding entitlement, and vice versa. If we have an obligation to repair a historical injustice, then there must be specific others – a community or particular individuals – who have an entitlement to reparation for that injustice. If a person or community has a reparative entitlement, then an individual or group must exist to whom the obligation to make repair can be assigned. Entitlement is the logical flip side of obligation, and from the specification of an obligation we can derive a statement about the corresponding entitlement.

Obligations, according to standard philosophical usage, are special moral duties that individuals or groups owe to others either because of a particular action or undertaking, or because they are in a special relationship. People acquire obligations when (for example) they sign a contract, make a promise, incur a debt, get married, or, as most people think, by being members of a family or citizens of a state (at least in those cases where family relationships are caring and states are reasonably just). Entitlements are, correspondingly, special rights that result from such actions or relationships. Obligations are different from our general duties as moral agents – for example, the duty to refrain from causing harm to others. Entitlements are different from rights we possess simply by virtue of being human. Everyone has general moral duties; everyone possesses human rights. Obligations and entitlements belong to particular individuals or groups at particular periods of time.

Obligations and entitlements can be moral or legal, or both. This study is about moral obligations and entitlements in respect to deeds

of the past, and thus it is only indirectly about historical responsibilities and entitlements in law. Nevertheless, legal concepts and ways
of thinking have had a profound influence on moral views concerning
reparation, compensation and related topics (and vice versa), and one
of the purposes of this study is to question, and find an alternative to,
the 'legalistic', or 'restorative', approach to reparation for historical
injustices.

Obligations and entitlements are duties or rights, 'all things being
equal'. They can be overridden by stronger moral claims. If fulfilling
my obligation to keep a promise means putting someone's life at risk,
then 'all things considered' it might be better not to keep it, and if so, I
should not be blamed for failing to do what I promised. Nor would I
usually be expected to keep a promise if an unanticipated change of
circumstances meant that keeping it would impoverish my family.
Obligations can come into conflict with each other or with general
moral duties, and this is especially likely to happen when obligations
are historical. Accepting an obligation to return land stolen by our
predecessors forces us to make a decision about how we should treat
the entitlements of those who are now in possession (if these entitlements exist). Fulfilling reparative obligations may clash with a duty to
make our society more equitable for all citizens. Determining what we
ought to do, all things considered, is often a difficult task. In some
cases there is no obviously right action, and people are likely to have
different opinions about what should be done. This investigation of
historical obligations and entitlements will not provide an answer to
all the moral and practical difficulties that people sometimes have to
face. Its aim is to present a position that addresses and resolves the
main problems posed by the existence of historical injustices.

Historical obligations encompass obligations arising from the
agreements or promises made by people of past generations as well
as obligations to make reparations for historical injustices. The first
chapter will discuss historical obligations created by treaties between
nations. But the primary focus of this study is on the entitlements
claimed by the successors or descendants of victims of injustice and
the obligations that are thought to be entailed by these claims. Such
obligations and entitlements belong to the subject matter of reparative
justice. Reparative justice concerns itself with what ought to be done
in reparation for injustice, and the obligation of wrongdoers, or their
descendants or successors, for making this repair. It is distinct from
retributive justice, which focuses on the punishment of wrongdoers,
and also from distributive justice – or 'justice as equity' – which tells
us how goods should be distributed among individuals or how
members of a society should share its benefits and burdens. There is

no consistent use of terms in discussions of reparative justice. I will use 'reparation' as a general term for all the ways in which the objectives of reparative justice can be achieved. 'Reparation' suggests repair – a fitting connotation for the theory I will advance. I will use the terms 'restitution' or 'restoration' for reparation that restores to victims, or their descendants or successors, goods that they have lost, and 'compensation' for reparation intended to provide victims, or their descendants or successors, either with some equivalent good or a benefit that makes up, to some extent, for the harm done. (However, the term 'compensation' has a more general use, as will be explained in chapter 3.)

Do we have historical obligations?

Reparative claims for historical injustices give rise to a host of difficult questions, but four seem particularly pressing. If they can be answered, other difficulties will become easier to resolve. The first task is to explain why historical obligations and entitlements exist. The dead cannot be restored to life, their suffering cannot be assuaged, or their possessions restored to them. Past people cannot be made to pay for the injustices they committed, and no one living should be punished for the deeds of the dead. The question naturally arises as to how descendants or successors of victims can be entitled to make demands, and why descendants or successors of perpetrators should be obliged to satisfy them. In refusing to apologize for historical injustices, the Australian Prime Minister is voicing a common response to reparative demands for historical injustices. Requiring that presently existing people make reparation for injustices done by their predecessors seems to many people to be not all that different from punishing people for crimes they did not commit.

Though it is common for people to deny that they have duties of reparation for historical injustices, there are historical obligations that almost everyone accepts. Most of us assume that government officials and citizens have an obligation (all things being equal) to keep treaties made by their predecessors. One way of breaking down the resistance to demands for reparation for historical injustices is to point this out. If citizens accept the obligation to honour treaties, and the sacrifices that this may entail, then why shouldn't they also accept the obligation to make reparation for past violations of treaties or, for that matter, for other historical injustices committed by officials of their state? Unfortunately, the persuasive power of this *ad hominem* argument is limited. Not everyone is likely to be convinced that an obligation to honour treaties entails accepting a reparative obligation for historical violations of treaties. In any case, when more closely scrutinized, the obligation to keep the treaties made by our predecessors is not as beyond question as it first appears. What gives a government the right to bind citizens of future generations to honour an agreement they had no part in making? Why should the democratic will of a people be limited by the agreements of their predecessors? A defence of historical obligations has to find an answer to these questions as well as a reply to doubts about more controversial claims.

In most philosophical discussions the existence of historical entitlements and obligations is predicated on the existence of 'historical titles' – that is, on historically acquired rights of property or possession that are passed on to people of succeeding generations. If someone takes possession of a good that was previously unowned, says Robert Nozick, then he or she has thereby acquired a right of possession. If she chooses to give or sell it to someone else, then by this act she transfers the entitlement to the recipient. If a person's right of possession is violated, then she has a right to 'rectification' – to be returned, so far as possible, to the situation that would have existed had the injustice not been done.[7] A historical entitlement to rectification exists, according to Nozick's account, if and only if someone's historical title has been unjustly violated. This person, or her descendants or successors, have a right to get back what was taken, or an equivalent in compensation.

One of the problems with this account of how people acquire historical entitlements and obligations is that it does not cover all cases where we are assigned historical responsibilities. It does not have anything to say about reparative responsibilities for injustices that do not involve violations of right of possession. Moreover, theories that depend on historical title are extremely controversial. Even if these titles exist, they may not justify a right to reparation for injustices that happened in previous generations. Should descendants of those who fled from Communist governments be allowed to claim the possessions of their forebears? Does a nation have legitimate claim to territory that was unjustly taken from it several centuries ago?

What is owed?

The issue of historical title is also central to the second question concerning historical entitlements and obligations: what, if anything, are we obliged to do about the injustices of the past? How do we determine the form or amount of reparation required? Nozick provides what appears to be a formula when he says that rectification demands a return to the situation that would have existed if the injustice had never been done or compensation equal in value to what was lost. If someone has stolen my bicycle, says Bernard Boxill, then justice demands that I get it back, or, if this is impossible, that I be given something I can regard as an equivalent, and that I should receive in addition payment for inconveniences caused to me by the theft.[8] Reparation, so understood, requires restoration, or at least compensation.

Reparation as restoration invites the question of what victims or their descendants can rightfully claim in cases of historical injustice. The bicycle owner ought to get his bicycle back. It is not so obvious that he can legitimately claim it twenty years after the theft has occurred, or that his descendants can do so.[9] There are other difficulties. Reparation as restoration applies at best to unjust dispossession or other violations concerning property, and not to injustices that may in fact loom larger in the minds of the victims or their descendants – murder, torture, enslavement, discrimination and denigration. Are these injustices simply beyond the scope of reparative justice? Is it an obscenity to offer money as recompense? The Jews who protested against Germany's offer of reparation to Holocaust survivors thought so.[10] Or should reparation take a different form? Unjust acts, Boxill insists, do not merely violate rights to possession. They are demonstrations of disrespect, and he thinks that reparation has to include 'an acknowledgment on the part of the transgressor that what he is doing is required of him because of his prior error', as well as the return, where possible, of whatever was unjustly taken.[11] He regards contrition in some form as a necessary component of reparation, and those who feel called upon to apologize for historical injustices appear to accept this idea.

Other ideas of what reparation should entail depart more radically from the idea of reparation as restoration. Apologies and other forms of reparation for historical injustice might be regarded as acts that look to the future rather than the past. Their purpose is, perhaps, to bring about a reconciliation between communities, to facilitate healing, to improve relationships between groups, to demonstrate a determination to act more justly in the future, to build an interpretation of the past that descendants of victims and perpetrators can share.[12] As accounts of the *meaning* of reparation, these suggestions are unacceptable. An apology or another act of reparation is an attempt to acknowledge and make amends for past injustice. If it were not so understood by its recipients – if they thought that it was being made only to make them feel better or to encourage their co-operation – they would regard it as insincere (and it probably would not have the desired effect). Nevertheless, the idea that reparative acts should be guided by forward-looking considerations is attractive. The difficult question is how this idea should be incorporated into a theory of reparation for historical injustices.

Reparation and equity

Historical entitlements and obligations are rights and duties, all things being equal. They may sometimes be outweighed by other moral considerations. It is even possible to suppose that they will *always* be outweighed by other considerations. The third major question for a theory about historical obligations and entitlements is what place, if any, they have in a more extensive theory of justice.

Some of those who think that historical entitlements ought to be played down or ignored are concerned about the bad consequences that can stem from dwelling on injustices of the past. It is all too easy to point to situations where preoccupation with historical grievances has encouraged enmities, resentment or acts of revenge. Others fear that obligations from the past are likely to interfere with what they believe to be the principal concern of justice: equitable distribution of goods according to the needs, deserts, preferences or choices of existing people. 'Why should not governments do what principles of equity require now rather than what outdated and often unprincipled agreements require?' says Will Kymlicka about treaties made with indigenous people.[13] David Lyons subscribes to this view when he invites us to view Indian land claims 'not as invoking an original right to land, a right that has been passed down to current Native Americans and that now needs to be enforced, but rather as an occasion for rectifying current inequities'.[14]

There are cases where it would be prudent to encourage people to put aside their reparative claims, and cases where the terms of past treaties should be ignored in favour of satisfying the needs of existing people. But it does not follow that it is always best to move forward rather than to look backward, or that removing unjust inequalities is all that matters. Many people care about the injustices of the past; they are inclined to think that something is owed in reparation for these wrongs, and they are predisposed to take reparative claims seriously. Those who make reparative claims for historical injustices assume that their demands have considerable moral force (as well as, in some cases, legal credibility). And there is reason to think that their perception is right. If I do someone a wrong – break a promise, for example – then I have an important and pressing obligation of reparation, an obligation that will not easily be trumped by other moral claims, even by the demands of justice as equity. The person I wronged would normally expect his claim on me to take priority over my general duty to provide benefits to others. So if historical entitlements to, and obligations for, reparation exist, then it is reasonable to presume that they will be of considerable importance. We would need good arguments for thinking that they ought to be ignored.

Let us assume then that historical obligations and entitlements have a significant role to play in a theory of justice. The question remains how they ought to be weighed against other duties, obligations and rights. In current debates about reparation for historical injustices, the principal dispute is between those who claim to have a reparative right to possessions of their forebears or predecessors and those who presently occupy or use these possessions. The claims of indigenous people to land taken from their ancestors are opposed by those who now farm, mine or live on this land and believe themselves to have a moral and legal right to keep it. Those who make reparative claims to houses and land in Eastern Europe are opposed by those who regard themselves as having a right based on occupancy and use. Most philosophical discussions of this issue either support the position taken by Nozick, that those who occupy property as the result of an injustice have no right to it, or support Lyons's view that the issue should be determined by reference to *existing* needs and inequities. Neither position seems satisfactory. It would be difficult to deny that present occupiers, people who themselves did no wrong and whose livelihood depends on possession, have some rights. But it is also difficult to deny the legitimacy of some of the reparative claims of indigenous people or others whose forebears were unjustly dispossessed. We have to find some way of adjudicating these opposing claims.

Ancient wrongs and current claims

The fourth question for a theory of historical obligations and entitlements inevitably arises in debates between claimants and present possessors: how far back into history are we required to go in search of wrongs to right? The British Prime Minister apologized for injustices committed against the Irish over a century ago. Should he also have apologized for the devastation caused by Cromwell's campaign against the Irish in the seventeenth century? 'Is the Greek government responsible for paying reparation to the descendants of Athenian helots? Would the descendants of a mill girl in Lowell, Massachusetts, who died of lint-lungs in 1845, have a claim on Washington, D.C. in 1965?' asks Robert Penn Warren.[15] He regards the absurdity of these claims as a *reductio ad absurdum* of all demands for reparation for historical injustices. Once we open the floodgates, he suggests, there is nothing to prevent all the injustices of history from swamping the courts and overtaxing our moral capacity. This is not a serious objection to attending to some of the injustices of the past. But even supporters of reparative claims have different ideas about how far back into history we ought to go. Boris Bittker agrees with Warren that slavery in the American South, though it may have been a legitimate focus for reparative claims in 1865, is too stale now to be a concern of justice.[16] But others disagree. Randall Robinson calls slavery a human rights crime that 'produces its victims *ad infinitum*, long after the active stage of the crime has ended'.[17] He has no doubt that demands for reparation for slavery are still justified.

What people say about the salience of more ancient injustices depends on the theory they use to justify reparative claims. If the only relevant issue for a theory of reparation is who can claim right of possession on the basis of a history of transfers (as Nozick believes), then passage of time ought to make no difference to the validity of claims – though in practice it may be impossible to determine who owes what to whom. On the other hand, those like Bittker, who think that reparation is owed only for existing harms, are more likely to discount ancient injustices. Bittker insists that it is not slavery that is responsible for the present disadvantages of African Americans, but the Jim Crow laws that enforced racial segregation in southern American states up into the 1960s.

Neither Nozick's nor Bittker's answer is satisfactory. Nozick's position not only depends on his controversial view about historical title. It fails to give due consideration to the effect of changes of circumstances and to the claims of those whose possession results from ancient injustices. Bittker's position does not acknowledge that ancient injustices often remain salient to descendants of the victims. Nor does it allow that some historical claims – like those of indigenous people for return of sacred or culturally important possessions – may resist extinction. Common sense suggests that temporal limitations have to be imposed on claims concerning historical injustices, but a theory of justice requires that this limitation not be arbitrary. We have to find a way of ruling out reparative claims like those derided by Robert Penn Warren, but we cannot reject without good reason the claim that reparation is owed for slavery, dispossession of indigenous peoples, and other relatively ancient injustices.

Historical obligations and transgenerational relationships

This study is a defence of historical obligation and entitlement. It will establish, first of all, that as members of nations and of other organized groups and communities we *do* have historical obligations. The fact that our predecessors or forebears were the ones who did the wrongs does not excuse us from a responsibility for reparation. It will treat these obligations as duties of justice and as requirements related to, but distinct from, the duty to undo presently existing inequities, and it will provide guidelines for determining who owes what to whom. In these respects it will conform to most conceptions of what a theory of reparation ought to do. But its method of justifying historical obligations and dealing with the difficulties associated with their existence will be different from most other treatments of the subject. The theory that I present does not depend on persisting historical titles. Nor does it deny requirements of equity, as Lyons or Kymlicka understand them. But it does not reject claims for reparation for historical injustices in favour of satisfying these other requirements. It gives historical injustices their due.

The approach I take to justification of historical obligations is grounded in a conception of a society or nation as an intergenerational community. Its institutions and moral relationships persist over time and through a succession of generations, and it depends for its moral and political integrity on its members accepting transgenerational obligations and honouring historical entitlements. The basic idea developed in the first two chapters can be simply stated. Members of such societies make, or think that they would be justified in making, moral demands on their successors. For example, they, or those who represent them, make commitments that are supposed to be binding on posterity and they think that their successors ought to honour these commitments. It is a basic meta-ethical principle that 'like cases should be treated alike': that those who impose a duty on others must be prepared to accept relevantly similar duties. By imposing obligations on their successors, or thinking that they would be justified in doing so, members of nations and other communities acquire obligations to fulfil similar responsibilities with respect to the commitments and relationships of their predecessors. They are morally required to maintain the practice of honouring the commitments of their predecessors (all things being equal) and to undertake other responsibilities associated with, or entailed by, the making of commitments. These include, I will argue, making reparation for past failures to honour commitments and for other injustices that demonstrated a lack of respect for other nations and their entitlements.

By insisting that reparation is owed for past injustices, this defence of historical obligation is backward-looking. But the justification contains forward-looking considerations. The existence of historical obligations is predicated on our moral relations to our successors. This way of thinking about historical obligations, as I will show, affects how we judge particular demands for reparation, and it provides a reason for accepting the 'reconciliatory' approach to reparative justice that I defend in chapter 3. The aim of reparation, according to 'reparation as reconciliation', is to repair relations damaged by injustice – not to return to a state of affairs that existed before the injustice was done. Reparation as reconciliation underwrites Boxill's idea that acknowledgement of wrong is an essential part of reparation. It also enables a theory of reparation to address the grievances and inequities that result from a particular history of injustice.

Historical entitlements and the claims of descendants of victims

Historical obligations belong to members of structured, intergenerational communities – groups capable of making and keeping transgenerational commitments. Those possessing historical entitlements are in many cases members of such communities, and in the first part of the study I focus on claims made by members of nations for reparation for past injustices to their community: for acts of aggression, expropriation of communal land, violation of sovereignty, breaking treaties, or destruction of communal life. There are, however, reparative claims of another kind that an account of historical entitlement must encompass – those made by individuals on their own behalf or on behalf of their family as descendants of victims of injustice. When Boxill insists that the descendants of slaves have a historical entitlement to reparation for the exploitation of their ancestors, he is not making a claim on behalf of the African-American nation. There is no such thing. The claim depends on the fact that African Americans are descendants of slaves.

Claims of this second kind raise the question of how individuals can be entitled to reparation for injustices that were done to others. Nozick's theory of historical title gives descendants of victims of injustice an entitlement that depends on their status as heirs of victims

of injustice – as individuals who would have acquired a possession if
the injustice had not been done. Others insist that descendants can
make a legitimate reparative claim when, and only when, they suffer
from the effects of a historical injustice. For example, Roy L. Brooks
insists that a 'meritorious redress claim' can be made only by those
who suffer harm causally connected to a past injustice.[18] Neither
avenue of justification seems promising. The first depends on a justification of the right of inheritance – a defence of what many social
theorists think is indefensible. The second raises many difficulties,
including one already mentioned: how do we determine what individuals would have had if an injustice had not been done? I will show in
the second part of this study that both ways of justifying reparative
claims become more defensible when they are viewed from the perspective of transgenerational relationships. Individuals who claim
reparations for historical injustices are not merely people who
happened to have been harmed by historical injustices or might
have been the recipients of possessions or benefits. They are the
descendants of victims of injustice. They are in a special relation
to those to whom the wrong was done. Highlighting this relationship
and the obligations and entitlements often associated with it, I
will argue, explains why descendants sometimes have a right of
inheritance, and also why they may be owed reparation for injustices
as ancient as slavery.

In each part of my study I concentrate on a few cases. The demand
of indigenous people for the return of expropriated tribal lands is the
example that features in my discussion of the historical entitlements
of nations. In my discussion of the entitlements of descendants of
victims of justice, I focus on the issue of whether white Americans
owe reparation for slavery and, if so, what form it should take. The
limitations of the study require that it have such a focus, but my
emphasis on these particular cases seems to leave me open to the
criticism that I am ignoring issues of great importance. What about
the reparative claims of Holocaust survivors and their descendants?
What about claims to territory made by nation-states on the basis of
historical possession? But the fact that I concentrate on particular
cases is not detrimental to the main purpose of the book. My intention is to present and defend a position that can be used to assess
many (if not all) of the reparative claims now being made. The theory
I advance is as relevant to the claims of descendants of Holocaust
survivors as the descendants of slaves, to the demands of nation-states
for historical possessions as the claims of indigenous people.

In the course of the argument that unfolds in the following chapters
I enter into debates about reparation and equity, rights of possession,

collective responsibility, and many other issues discussed by philosophers. However, the subject matter of this investigation is not merely academic. It addresses the urgent moral problems raised by demands that are becoming more prevalent and insistent. As such, it is a contribution to practical morality and to a politics concerned with the age-old question of what is just.

PART I

Obligations
of Nations and
Rights of Reparation

1

Treaties and Transgenerational Responsibilities

Assembled Maori chiefs and a representative of the British government signed an agreement at Waitangi on the North Island of New Zealand in February 1840. Maoris ceded governance of New Zealand in return for protection from settlers and foreign invaders. The treaty guaranteed to Maoris control over their lands and traditional hunting and fishing rights. Less than a decade later the colonial government gave in to the demands of settlers and allowed them to encroach on Maori land. Armed resistance by the Maoris provided a justification for seizing more Maori land and revoking their communal rights. By the end of the century the Chief Justice of the colony had declared the treaty a 'simple nullity'. This perception was changed during the 1980s by a campaign of Maoris and their supporters, who demanded that the government acknowledge the rights guaranteed to Maori communities by the Treaty of Waitangi and return land unjustly taken.[1]

This history tells a familiar story. The Cherokee of Georgia and North Carolina were guaranteed their tribal lands by a treaty signed in 1684, but incursions by settlers resulted in losses of land which were 'legalized' in one treaty after another. In spite of a ruling in favour of the Indians by a federal court, the American government, urged into action by local officials, decided on a forced removal of the whole Cherokee population. The people were rounded up and marched under armed guard out of their remaining territory and forced to settle on the other side of the Mississippi. This march of the Cherokee to Oklahoma – the 'Trail of Tears' – resulted in the death of at least one-quarter of the tribe.[2] Cherokee communities are still trying to obtain reparation for this and other wrongs.

Treaties as promises

Governments, most people agree, should keep their promises. Promises, to be sure, are obligations, all things being equal. The law and common sense allow that there can be good excuses for not keeping an agreement: it may have been made under duress or in ignorance; it may be vitiated by unforeseen circumstances or moral considerations. However, it is difficult to suppose that the British Crown, or the New Zealand and American governments that inherited its powers and responsibilities, had a legitimate excuse for what they did.[3] These and many other violations of treaties made with indigenous people were injustices. They were not the only injustices done to members of indigenous communities. Aborigines of Australia and indigenous peoples of America and Canada were slaughtered and denied protection by the law; their cultures and means of life were systematically destroyed in the course of European settlement. But treaty violations provide an obvious test case for accounts of historical obligation. The basic question posed by those who demand a return to the terms of the Treaty of Waitangi is raised by all demands for the repair of past injustices: what, if anything, are people now obliged to do about repairing a historical wrong?

Defending historical obligations, as I have pointed out, requires explaining why people now living can have a responsibility for keeping promises they did not make or repairing injustices they did not commit. In the case of treaties and treaty violations this seems like an easy task. A treaty, as the Vienna Convention on the Law of Treaties makes clear, is a contract and brings with it the same moral and legal assumptions that surround promise or contract making.[4] A treaty is a promise of state. 'A treaty is intended to be of perpetual duration and incapable of unilateral termination,' says an authority on international law.[5] Legal conventions treat states like individuals and assign them the same responsibilities for their commitments as individual persons are supposed to have for theirs. The state is responsible for honouring its agreements and for any of the breaches that its officials commit. Since the state consists of its citizens, past, present and future, this responsibility devolves on whoever is in the position to assume it. Most citizens accept this.

Treaties made with indigenous people have not been recognized traditionally in international law, but there is no reason for doubting that they too had the moral force of promises. They too were commitments made by political communities to each other, and were supposed to be valid 'so long as the grass is green and the sky is blue'. The fact that agents of government or colonial administrators were often deceitful and did not mean to keep their promises did not invalidate the agreements they made. An insincere promise is nevertheless a promise. Indigenous communities were not states, but they were independent or semi-independent societies with a political structure and governed by law – and many people refer to them as 'nations'. The British Crown made an agreement with Maori nations, and this agreement, according to conventional understanding, has been inherited by the New Zealand nation. The British Crown, and later the United States, made many treaties with Indian nations.

This way of speaking may strike some people as absurd. Maoris are New Zealand citizens, and Cherokees are Americans. If by signing the Treaty of Waitangi the Maoris became British subjects, how can they have retained their own nations? How can a community of New Zealanders or Americans make a claim on behalf of their nation against their nation? This problem is largely terminological. A nation, as I will define it, is a self-governing society or community with the power to make laws for itself (at least concerning its domestic affairs) and to make agreements with other such societies. Nations sometimes contain subordinate nations within their borders – societies that are subject in some respects to the law of the superior power, but retain some of the political entitlements of nations. Canada and the United States are nations (nation-states) that have within their borders semi-independent Indian nations with an entitlement, limited by constitutional requirements, to govern their own affairs. A nation, according to my definition, is a political society – not a cultural or religious group (though members of a nation may share a culture or a religion) – and a person can be a member of more than one nation.[6] Leaders of nation-states and their legislatures represent on most occasions all their citizens; but in their dealings with semi-independent nations within their borders, they represent people who can be regarded as belonging to a nation distinct from their nation-state. They represent Pakeha (non-Maori) New Zealanders, or Americans or Canadians who are not Indians. To claim that New Zealand is responsible for keeping the Treaty of Waitangi is to speak of it as such a nation. Difficulties can arise about the membership of nations or about their identity through time. There can be borderline cases – communities that have lost so much of their political structure and law that it is difficult to regard them as nations. I will discuss some of these problems in later chapters. But in many cases there are no grounds for denying that the indigenous nation that was party to a historical agreement continues to exist, or that there is a nation which can rightfully claim to be the inheritor of the political legacy of the nation that made the agreement.

Nations ought to keep their agreements (all things being equal), and their liability for treaty violations seems to follow from the responsibilities they assume when they make commitments. The problem is that nations are not really individuals. Their policies and commitments depend on the actions and intentions of real individuals – as leaders, officials and citizens. A nation can be said to make a treaty because those individuals who count as the appropriate officials have entered into negotiations and reached agreement, and others have ratified this agreement according to accepted procedures. If the treaty is kept, this is because officials and citizens are prepared to perform the required actions and refrain from violations. Keeping a treaty can be burdensome. It can require citizens to forego significant advantages. It can force them to go to war to defend a treaty partner. Individuals who demand a moral justification for the burdens imposed on them are not being unreasonable. We cannot simply assume that it is morally legitimate to pass on obligations and entitlements from members of one generation to another. This is precisely what needs to be justified.

A nation, it might be insisted, just *is* a political organization that makes transgenerational agreements. Treaty making and keeping is essential to its nature, and all its members have to accept this. However, a nation is a human artefact. What it is or does is determined by the actions and interests of its members, and those who refuse to accept the burdens imposed on them by treaties from the past are not making a conceptual error. They are questioning the terms of their association – something they surely have a right to do. The response to their objections might appeal to prudence. If citizens were not prepared to keep the agreements of their predecessors (at least sometimes), then long-term commitments between nations would be impossible. But long-term agreements are often a good thing. They tend to promote trust and peaceful coexistence. So reluctant citizens might be persuaded that the burdens they are forced to assume are justified because of these good consequences. However, this reasoning is not so likely to persuade them if the benefits of violating an agreement are considerable, or if the burdens of keeping it are onerous. They will be particularly unimpressed if the injured party is not in a position to retaliate effectively or if the motivation behind the agreement was to practice deceit. But the real problem with prudential justifications for treaty keeping is not that the arguments may fail to convince. They do not explain why citizens have an obligation to keep treaties just because their predecessors made them. They do not treat treaties as promises.[7]

If prudential justifications for keeping treaties of predecessors are not satisfactory, then what other reasons can we appeal to? The problem of justifying historical obligations bears a resemblance to what has been called the 'problem of political obligation' – the problem of explaining why citizens should support the institutions of their nation, obey its laws, and other requirements. The problem arises because it is commonly assumed that the authority of the nation rests on the consent of its citizens. But most of us have never consented to the authority of our nation, or voluntarily accepted the burdens of citizenship. These were thrust upon us by an accident of birth.

Nevertheless, there are some notable differences between the problem of political obligation and the difficulties raised by historical obligation. One of them is that political obligation is not a real issue – at least not for most people in relatively just, democratic nations. Most of us accept the authority of our laws and national institutions without wondering whether our nation has a right to make demands of us. But whether citizens have historical obligations is a live issue. Controversies raised by demands for reparation show that many people do not think that they have a responsibility for paying the moral debts of their political predecessors. Another difference is that the way in which our national institutions exercise authority over us can, at least in a democracy, be affected by what we do. We can collectively change the law or even the constitution; we can rebuild institutions to suit our needs. The control that we can exercise over our political existence is probably one reason why most of us are willing to accept the authority of our laws and institutions. But a historical obligation to keep treaties or make reparation for past violations cannot be abrogated or altered – even by the combined will of citizens. So historical obligations are going to seem objectionable not only to those who regard forced obedience as an imposition on their lives as free beings, but also to those proponents of democracy who think that citizens should collectively be able to determine what burdens they will assume.[8]

So it is not illogical for people to accept political authority, even to have a strong sense of loyalty to their nation or fellow members, and yet reject historical obligations. They may acknowledge obligations to present and future members. They may agree that they have a duty to keep agreements of officials who represent them and to make reparation for wrongs their leaders and representatives have committed.[9] But they can at the same time deny that they have an obligation to fulfil historical agreements or make reparations for deeds done before they were born, came of age, or arrived in the country. This means that solving the problem of political obligation, or denying that the problem really exists, would not necessarily resolve difficulties concerning historical obligations and entitlements.

Obligation and historical title

The problem of explaining why we have a historical obligation to keep agreements made by our predecessors might be avoided altogether if Nozick is right about historical title. If the Maoris have a persisting entitlement to their land, then those who now occupy it have an obligation to give it back (or provide appropriate compensation). A treaty, it could be argued, is merely a political means of protecting basic rights, and thus not philosophically all that interesting. The right to land would remain even if the treaty had never existed.[10]

One problem with this argument is that treaties are made for many purposes: for protection against attack, to ensure co-operation, to co-ordinate activities, etc. So the existence of morally basic titles to land would not relieve us of the task of explaining why we ought to keep the agreements of our predecessors. It could be said that, by putting us into a special relation with members of another nation, *every* treaty generates obligations that are likely to have implications for the way in which we discharge our responsibilities or how we should behave if we fail. Treaties are not morally superfluous. But the more serious difficulty with appeals to historical titles is that they may not be so morally basic as their supporters suppose. Nozick assumes that we should argue from entitlements to obligations: since he believes that individuals and groups have a persisting title to their possessions, he insists that we have an obligation to ensure that this right is not violated, or if violated to rectify the situation. But the direction of the argument might be reversed: 'Because we do not have an obligation to rectify the wrongs of our predecessors, persisting historical titles (like that claimed by the Maori) do not exist.' Those who refuse to think that they have such an obligation will be predisposed to argue in this way. Barring a convincing and strong reason for the existence and persistence of the entitlement, what is to prevent them from doing so?[11]

Collective responsibility and the past

Since keeping treaties and making reparations for past violations are supposed to be the collective responsibility of individuals as citizens, or citizens of a certain kind, it is natural to look to theories about collective responsibility to explain why historical obligations exist. But most accounts of why members have moral responsibilities for activities of their group reinforce the idea that there is no obligation without participation. These theories have the objective of determining whether, and to what extent, individuals are responsible for the deeds of their leaders or other members of their group – whether, for example, ordinary citizens bear some responsibility for the involvement of their country in an unjust war. Almost all of them agree that it would be unjust to hold individuals liable for actions which they had no possibility of influencing. Joel Feinberg, for example, lists 'opportunity for control' as one of the necessary conditions for liability for an action or practice of a group.[12] A citizen of a democracy – even one who doesn't vote or pay attention to politics – may bear some responsibility for the wrongs done by officials of her nation. She could have been more informed and politically active, she could have spoken out against injustice. But she had no way of influencing the actions of members of past generations – no way of objecting to agreements they made or injustices they did.

If moral responsibility depends on liability, and liability on control or ability to participate, then historical obligations do not exist. However, defenders of historical obligation often have in mind a different idea of how members of collectives acquire responsibilities. The wealth of nations has been built on past injustices. Non-indigenous Americans, Australians, New Zealanders, South Africans and Canadians are now benefiting from injustices done to indigenous communities – from the consequences of broken treaties, from land that was seized and settled.

> If the Aborigines had not lost their land, and had maintained their traditional relationship with the land on which their well-being depended, then white Australian society could not have developed in the way it has, whites would not enjoy the high levels of well-being they enjoy, Aborigines would not have suffered significant losses in self-esteem, and nor would they have been so culturally devastated.[13]

The beneficiaries of this injustice, Bigelow, Pargetter and Young go on to say, have a duty to repair the injuries suffered by the victims.

There are two ways of understanding this claim. According to the first, beneficiaries of historical injustices are the receivers of stolen goods. They have been unjustly enriched. Justice demands the return of these goods to their rightful owners, or at least compensation in some form. The second says that those who have gained through interactions should share their benefits with those who have suffered loss. The fact that the losses suffered by indigenous people are the result of wrongs done by a nation plays no essential role in the argument so understood. Beneficiaries would have just as strong a reason for sharing if their gains, and the losses of others, had been the result of economic or natural contingencies for which no one could have been blamed. If, for example, the normal economic interactions of people of a nation result in the collapse of a large business and unemployment for its workers, then many of us believe that those who have benefited from these interactions should provide compensation in the form of unemployment benefits and other subsidies for those who have suffered the harm. Graduated income tax is supposed to ensure that those who benefit the most bear the greatest burden. But there is no question of blaming them for the harm, and no reason to think of their payments as reparation. What this second interpretation of the argument calls for, in other words, is compensation for unfair disadvantage – not reparation for wrong done. Compensation for losses incurred as the result of social interactions is required by many theories of equity, so the common belief that beneficiaries of past injustices owe something to people who have been harmed is probably best interpreted in this way.[14]

The argument from unjust enrichment *does* insist that beneficiaries of injustice have a historical obligation of reparation, and would have this obligation even if they had not prospered from their ill-got gains (and even if the victims or their descendants were relatively prosperous). But the idea that such an obligation exists seems to depend on the existence and persistence of historical titles. If the land of their ancestors still belongs to the Maori, then, according to the argument, the present inhabitants are benefiting from something that does not belong to them. The problem is not merely that the argument from unjust enrichment makes an assumption about the persistence of title that many people are inclined to question. It also ignores claims that present inhabitants might make on their own behalf. The existence of Maori title does not exclude the possibility that present possessors may also have an entitlement. It is notable that the law puts limitations on what can be claimed in restitution, and for how long.[15] If many years have passed since the theft occurred, the claim of the original owner is likely to lapse, and that of the present possessor will take precedence. There is in fact a good reason for imposing limitations on entitlement to restitution. We generally assume that those who obey the law and act justly have the right to pursue their projects, engage in commercial activities and enjoy the fruits of their labour without the fear that they will be stripped of their possessions because of an injustice committed by others a long time ago.[16] Those who react with indignation to reparation claims, who regard them as 'unfair', may do so for this reason.

Guilt, shame, and identity

The ideas of collective responsibility so far examined seem to ignore an important psychological fact. People sometimes do feel guilt or shame for injustices committed by members of their group, or are made uncomfortable by the knowledge that they are benefiting from past injustice. Many citizens are sorry for the wrongdoing of their predecessors and are prepared to take responsibility for keeping their agreements. An account of collective responsibility that takes these responses seriously is likely to be in a much better position to justify historical obligations.

Alasdair MacIntyre thinks that the explanation for such responses comes from the fact that we are bearers of a particular social identity.

> I am someone's son or daughter, someone else's cousin or uncle...I belong to this clan, that tribe, this nation. Hence what is good for me has to be the good for one who inhabits these roles. As such I inherit from the past of my family, my city, my tribe, my nation, a variety of debts, inheritances, rightful expectations and obligations. These constitute the given of my life, my moral starting point.

The self, he says, has a history that stretches back before birth. And he contrasts this 'narrative view of the self' with the viewpoint of modern individualism which detaches the self from all social relationships and denies that a person can be held responsible for 'what his father did or for what his country does or has done'.[17] The modern individualist is likely to deny historical obligations, but those with a narrative view of themselves cannot.

MacIntyre's presents a 'strong' account of collective responsibilities in the sense that he makes them follow from an identity with, or commitment to, a community. It claims that we have a relation to our community that entails special responsibilities, including historical obligations. The 'weak' position of Feinberg, on the other hand, does not presuppose the existence of special community obligations. It makes our collective responsibilities follow from a general human duty to promote justice and prevent unjust actions of the groups to which we happen to belong. It is not a theory about political or communal obligation. A strong theory seems attractive, because it solves several problems at once. It purports to explain why we have special duties to our community or nation, and also why we should assume responsibility for communal deeds that we had no possibility of influencing.

MacIntyre makes a person's special obligations depend on the nature of his or her self. But not all selves are narrative selves, and those that are will tell many different stories. MacIntyre himself thinks that individualist selves are becoming more common in the modern (or post-modern) world, but these are the people most likely to deny that they have communal or historical obligations. Even those who do regard themselves as attached in an essential way to others are likely to have different ideas about which relationships form their identity. Some people regard their family as central to their lives, but have little interest in their nation. The immigrant may continue to derive his self-identity from the land of his ancestors and have no feeling of responsibility for the inheritance of his new nation. Nor does acceptance of responsibility necessarily follow from identification. A person can locate herself within a history or identify with a group without thinking that she is obliged to do anything about the commitments or injustices of past people. And there is no necessary connection between feeling shame or regret for the sins of predecessors and taking responsibility for reparation. MacIntyre's narrative view of the self can account for why some people are prepared to take responsibility for the past of their community, but it is not able to establish that all members of nations should accept historical obligations.

Perhaps these obligations arise simply from the fact that we are members of certain kinds of community. If so, they are basic duties, ones that people are supposed to accept without asking for reasons.[18] Most people do take for granted that they have family obligations – responsibilities to brothers and sisters, parents and children, even to uncles and aunts. They accept such duties even though family membership is not a matter of choice, and even when they do not have positive feelings about all their relatives. Many people are also prepared to accept national responsibilities as a matter of course. But if people are supposed to accept these obligations without asking for reasons, then it is difficult to see what arguments can be given to someone who has different ideas about duty or different loyalties. Accusations of immorality are likely to be perceived by non-conformists as moral bullying. Nor does acceptance of communal obligations necessarily require taking responsibility for the past. We can accept obligations to members of our own family – those with whom we live or interact – without supposing that we have an obligation to pay the debts of our parents, let alone more distant ancestors. We can acknowledge special obligations to members of our nation without supposing that we have historical obligations for its past.

The possibility remains that we acquire commitments and obligations, including obligations with respect to the past, through participation in communal activities. Margaret Gilbert thinks that a joint commitment comes into existence when people participate in joint activities or signal their readiness to participate. Having shown through their actions that they have entered a commitment, they constitute with others a plural subject and acquire responsibilities for fulfilling its intentions.[19] Most of Gilbert's examples of joint commitment focus on personal relations. By using conventional gestures or words to signal that I accept an invitation to dance, I thereby commit myself to forming a dance-floor couple. But she thinks that we also acquire joint commitments as members of more enduring plural subjects like nations. We signal our readiness by participating in public events, voting in elections, or even by our use of language – by the use of 'we', as in 'We are engaged in a war against terrorism'.

Once individuals have committed themselves to being part of such a plural subject, they acquire responsibility for its deeds. Having this responsibility does not depend on participation, and lack of culpability is no reason for denying obligation. Since a nation is an ongoing, intergenerational, plural subject, joint commitment means sharing responsibility for its past. Gilbert wants to explain why people sometimes feel guilty for what their nation has done, even when they bear no responsibility as individuals. But her position also implies that people who don't feel guilt may nevertheless have obligations, including historical obligations, as citizens.

There is a large gap, however, between personal relations that give rise to legitimate expectations and the relations of individuals in a large, impersonal society.[20] In face-to-face interactions people can make their intentions clear, especially if they are able to rely on mutually understood conventions. The mere fact that people participate in public events or use 'we' when speaking of the nation is not enough to establish that they are participants in a joint commitment. Even if these activities did indicate commitment, they would not tell us what responsibilities people have accepted, or exactly whom they are committed to. They may be signalling a commitment to the people of their nation, but not a readiness to fulfil the intentions of its leaders, still less to take responsibility for what leaders or officials did in the past.

Are there actions that do signal such a commitment? Expressing pride in the past deeds of the nation may be one. 'Can one accept the benediction and reject the curse? Can one accept the legacy and avoid the duty of paying its debts?'[21] But this point, though it may be correct, does not get us very far. We have returned to the problems associated with MacIntyre's conception of the narrative self. Having responsibility is made to depend on a response that many people belonging to a nation – recent immigrants, for example – may not share. And worse, it is not a response that requires any particular action.

This brief discussion of views about collective responsibility is not exhaustive. Nor am I likely to have proved to everyone's satisfaction that the views of MacIntyre, Gilbert and others are not able to do the job of explaining why we have historical obligations. However, the problems encountered by common, and not so common, views about collective responsibility for historical injustices are reason enough to search for an alternative.

Presuppositions of promising

The first step is to explain why presently existing citizens or members of nations are obliged to keep the treaties of their predecessors. Understanding why this historical obligation exists will put us in a better position to understand why citizens have an obligation to make reparations for historical violations of agreements and for wrongs other than treaty violations.

All arguments begin with assumptions. I will take it for granted that the Vienna Convention on the Law of Treaties rightly regards a treaty as having the legal and moral force of a promise or contract. A promise is supposed to *entitle* those to whom it is made to trust that it will be kept. Violation of a treaty, like violation of a promise, is the breaking of a trust – which counts as an injustice even if the recipient of the promise does not suffer loss. The obligation to keep a promise is a duty, all things being equal, and a complete account of promise or treaty making would have to define the circumstances that would make commitments void or inapplicable (as the Vienna Convention does in its codification of international conventions concerning treaties). But in the absence of such circumstances it is assumed that nations ought to honour their agreements.

Treaty violations are common occurrences in the affairs of nations. But this does not detract from their moral force. Indeed, the very existence of a treaty system depends on the prevalence, at least as a guiding idea, of what the convention calls 'good faith'. 'Every treaty in force is binding upon the parties to it and must be performed by them in good faith.'[22]

I will also assume that citizens of democratic nations, or nations that provide their members with some means of influencing the behaviour of leaders or governments, are collectively responsible for the policies and political actions of their representatives and officials. This includes a collective responsibility for keeping the agreements that their representatives make. The issue is how these citizens can have an obligation to honour agreements that were made not by their representatives, but by leaders and officials of the past. I do not assume any particular account of why citizens have collective responsibilities. They might be thought of as arising from the influence that citizens can exercise over their leaders – the view of collective responsibility promoted by orthodox theories. Or they may be regarded as a consequence of social identity or the commitment of citizens to each other or to the nation itself. Strong accounts of collective responsibility, as we have seen, do not relieve us of the task of justifying historical obligations. But a weaker account will suffice.

What makes treaties possible?

By their nature treaties are 'posterity-binding': they are meant to impose obligations on our political successors as well as ourselves. To be perpetually valid, or even valid for a reasonable period of time, a treaty has to bind citizens of the future. Those with whom it is made are being given an entitlement to trust that this will be so. This means that if we endorse such an agreement, then we must suppose that our successors have an obligation to keep it – at least so long as it can be regarded as applicable and fair. But how is it possible to impose obligations on our successors? The problem is not merely that our control over what future people will do is limited – that we will not be in a position to force them to do what we want. The primary issue is moral. What gives us the moral entitlement to perform an act that imposes obligations on future people? What gives those with whom we have made an agreement the entitlement to trust that our commitment binds our successors? And why should these future people regard themselves as bound by our agreements? Only by answering these questions, can we understand what makes treaties as promises possible. Let us tackle each of them in turn.

Suppose that through our elected representatives we want to make a posterity-binding treaty with another community. Let us assume that everyone concerned is sincere and morally responsible. We intend to keep the agreement, and have the capacity to do so. But our sincerity and our situation are not sufficient to give us the right to undertake something on behalf of our successors. A moral entitlement to make such a posterity-binding commitment, I suggest, depends on this act taking place within the framework of a moral practice that requires us to take responsibility for fulfilling posterity-binding commitments of our political predecessors.

That this is so follows from a basic assumption about morality, at least in those cases where we are reasoning about public affairs – that 'like cases ought to be treated alike'. If you assign duties or obligations to others, then you have to be prepared to accept the same (or relevantly similar) duties yourself. If you insist that others should refrain from throwing their litter on the street, then you have to believe that you and your friends are under the same obligation. If you deny that this duty is also yours, then you do not have the moral authority to tell others what they ought to do. In other words, making a legitimate moral demand means conforming to a practice requiring (among other things) that you accept that the same judgement would apply to anyone who was in a relevantly similar situation, including yourself. Moral prescriptions associated with treaty making are different in one respect from more familiar judgements about what people in a particular position ought to do. The people on whom we are imposing duties are our national successors, not just our contemporaries. This means that 'treating like cases alike' commits us to accepting similar obligations in cases where *we* are the successors.[23]

Being willing to accept as an obligation a demand made by our predecessors is not, to be sure, sufficient to ground a posterity-binding obligation. Suppose people demand that their successors take revenge on the people of those nations that have done them an injury. They are prepared to conform to the 'treat like cases alike' rule and take revenge on the people who injured *their* predecessors. But their demand gives rise to no obligation. Their successors can ignore their wishes, and so they should. Revenge is not a good idea from a moral point of view, particularly when it is being visited on people who were not themselves responsible for an injury. This means that we, as responsible moral agents, do not regard it as legitimate to demand of our successors that they take revenge on our enemies, and thus we have no obligation to heed calls for revenge made by our predecessors. What we demand of our successors must be something we can regard as morally legitimate. This is a presupposition for the application of the rule. For the same reason we are not entitled to insist that our successors keep unfair promises, and have no obligation to honour the unfair promises of our predecessors. But if a promise is fair (and satisfies the other conditions associated with promising), then no moral considerations stand in the way of us binding our successors. (Indeed, I will argue in the next chapter that we cannot reasonably avoid making posterity-binding commitments.)

Why not say that the possibility of making a posterity-binding commitment requires only that we take steps to ensure that our successors will carry it out? We could make a law designed to force them to do this, or even enshrine the treaty in the constitution of our political society. Making treaties into law is in fact a standard practice in many countries. We could indoctrinate our children to honour our commitments. The problem with these measures however, is not merely that they might fail. The issue is not the effectiveness of the means we might use to induce our successors to do what we want. What needs to be explained is how we can presume an entitlement to impose a *moral* obligation on our successors. What gives us the authority to say that they *ought* to honour our agreements? The answer is that our moral authority comes from accepting the obligation to honour the morally acceptable agreements of our predecessors.

We reach the same conclusion when we look at the matter from the point of view of those with whom we make an agreement. We want them to be able to trust that it will be fulfilled. But our sincerity, our own ability to keep the agreement, and the moral reasonableness of the agreement itself do not give them a sufficient reason for trust. It is not only our own willingness to fulfil the undertaking that is in question, but its acceptance as an obligation by our successors. Those with whom the agreement is made are entitled to trust us only if they also have good reason to believe that they are dealing with a people who accept the moral practice of honouring the agreements of their predecessors.

Let us assume that we are entitled to make our posterity-binding commitment. Why should our political successors think that they are obliged to keep it? They may, of course, think that the agreement suits their purposes and abide by its terms for this reason. But in this case they aren't really *honouring* our agreement. They are merely doing what they see to be in their interests. They would not keep it if it were not so convenient. Their *obligation* to keep our agreements arises from their belief that the agreements they make ought to be honoured by *their* successors. By committing their successors to honour their agreements, they take on the responsibility of honouring ours. They are obliged to accept the consequences of their practice.

This explanation of why we have a historical obligation to honour treaties made by our predecessors may seem like an unnecessarily complicated way of defending what almost everyone concedes: that nations ought to keep their promises. The complexity is justified by special problems raised by historical obligations and the fact that other ways of dealing with these problems do not seem adequate. My account does not depend on the identification of citizens with people of the past. Nevertheless, it obliges them to see themselves as participants in a transgenerational relationship in which each generation inherits obligations from its predecessors and passes on obligations to its successors. The implications and advantages of this approach will be explored in later chapters, when my account of historical obligation takes on difficult cases. But first it has to answer some obvious objections.

Intentions and obligations

Treaty keeping is a backward-looking obligation, but the justification I have offered is forward-looking in the sense that it depends on the concern of morally responsible citizens that their commitments be honoured by their successors. For this reason it might be accused of the same inadequacy as the prudential view that I criticized earlier in this chapter – that it does not provide a plausible account of why people are obligated to honour promises and contracts. Suppose we don't make any posterity-binding promises at all. Does this mean that we are relieved of the responsibility of honouring the promises of our predecessors?

The answer is 'No'. Our moral commitments do not depend on what we actually do or refrain from doing. They depend on our judgements about what ought to be done in cases real or merely possible. Much of our moral reasoning is hypothetical. We make judgements about what we would be morally obliged to do if a particular situation *were* to occur. The point of such an exercise is to identify those moral practices to which we are committed. The moral practice we think we ought to adopt in relation to the promises of our predecessors is determined not by whether we actually make posterity-binding promises, but by what we think our successors ought to do were we to make them.

I have been assuming in this discussion that we are morally responsible citizens, that we intend to adhere to the morally acceptable agreements that our representatives have made, and think that our successors should do so too. But suppose we are not so conscientious. Suppose that our motivations are less sincere, and our intentions more devious. We do not intend to keep our agreement, or perhaps we intend to keep it only so long as it serves our interests. We certainly have no desire to bind our successors. Does this mean that we avoid incurring an obligation to honour the commitments of our predecessors? Does it mean that our successors have no obligation to honour the agreement? The issue raised by this last question is particularly relevant to our actual situation. For we have good reason to believe that in many cases our predecessors had no intention of honouring the treaties they made with indigenous people and had no desire that we do so. The many treaties made with the Cherokee were devices for 'legalizing' invasions of their territory, and no one could have believed that the American government intended to prevent further incursions. Some of the British officials who promulgated the Treaty of Waitangi may have been sincere, but others probably thought of it as a device for placating savages until Her Majesty's forces arrived in greater strength. In many cases the motivations of our predecessors are unknown, and now unknowable.

Do people who do not intend that their posterity-binding agreements be kept have a duty to honour the posterity-binding treaties of their predecessors? The answer is, obviously, 'Yes'. People do not avoid having duties by being immoral. If I make a promise with no intention of keeping it, I am not relieved of obligations. I open myself up to accusations of insincerity and abusing the trust of others. People who make a posterity-binding agreement without intending that it be kept are equally immoral. They are pretending to conform to a practice that requires that they and their successors honour a promise. They incur the obligations that this practice entails, whether or not they intend to fulfil them. Reasoning from the perspective of a morally responsible person is not merely a way of determining what rules or practices a morally responsible person should follow. It provides a standard for criticizing the behaviour of those who are less responsible – and for making judgements about what they ought to have done.

Do we have an obligation to fulfil promises that our predecessors did not intend us to keep? The answer depends on how we interpret the 'treat like cases alike' requirement: whether it requires us to fulfil the *intentions* of our predecessors or to keep their *promises*. How we interpret this rule depends in turn on what we, as morally responsible citizens, think that our successors should do. The answer seems clear. We want them to honour our agreements not because this is what we intend them to do – not out of regard for our desires or other psychological states – but because we think our agreements should be honoured. The trust of those who have made an agreement with us should not be violated. In other words, we are assigning our successors an obligation to honour our commitments, not a duty to fulfil our intentions. So the appropriate and relevant description of our obligation in respect to the agreements of our predecessors is to fulfil their promises. Their intentions, good or bad, are not relevant – at least not to the determination of what it means to treat like cases alike. What is morally important is not the state of mind of those who made a commitment, but the fact that it was made.

The same conclusions follow if we reason about the matter from the point of view of those with whom an agreement is made – if we put ourselves in their position, as the 'treat like cases alike' rule demands that we do. If we were those to whom a commitment was made, we would believe ourselves to be entitled to trust that it would be kept. We would believe ourselves entitled to engage in undertakings or make plans for the future with the understanding that the agreement would be upheld, not only by those who made it but also by their successors. We would be prepared to accept some excuses for not keeping the agreement; but we would not regard it as acceptable if these successors refused to honour it on the grounds that their predecessors were insincere and did not intend it to be kept.

This way of reasoning about our historical obligations has the obvious advantage of relieving us of problems associated with the intentions of past people. It does not require us to respect or fulfil their intentions. It does not require that we know what their intentions were. Moreover, it puts us in a good position to deal with another problem concerning intentions. A question that often arises when dealing with agreements from the past is how we should interpret their terms or determine their validity. Should we interpret and apply them according to the intentions of those who made them (so far as we know what they were)? To do so may require us to act in ways we think to be unjust – either because the terms of the agreement were meant to favour the interests of the powerful, or because circumstances have changed, or because our predecessors' conception of justice was different from ours. Should we interpret and apply the agreement, so far as we can, according to contemporary ideas of justice? But if so, then surely we are simply doing what we happen to regard as just and not keeping the promises of our predecessors.

In order to be said to be keeping an agreement, we have to refer to its provisions and provide an interpretation of what they were supposed to protect or guarantee. But my account of why we have an obligation to keep the agreements of our predecessors favours the idea that the interpretation and application of these provisions should depend on what we now think is fair. We think our successors ought to keep our commitments not simply because these commitments were made, but because we regard the terms as just. But we know that circumstances change and that our ideas about justice are not above criticism. The duty we assign to our successors is thus to interpret and apply our agreements in a just way according to the circumstances. We have the same obligation with respect to the agreements of our predecessors. Suppose, for example, a treaty our predecessors made with an indigenous nation gave them fishing rights in a particular area. Because of ecological changes for which no one is directly responsible, the fish have moved away to an area beyond that designated by the treaty. The indigenous people are still dependent on fishing for their livelihood. We might under these circumstances interpret the treaty as guaranteeing a source of livelihood for indigenous people, and thus apply it by ceding them the new fishing ground. Controversies about what is just are bound to arise in this and other cases. But the issues can be settled only by appealing to present circumstances and the ideas of justice that people now have.

We are entitled to interpret the agreements of our predecessors according to our ideas of justice, even though we know that our predecessors had somewhat different ideas. Our conception of justice is for us what justice is, and we are entitled to judge according to our moral convictions. We are entitled, for example, to insist that slavery was unjust, even though we know that some of our predecessors saw nothing wrong with it. So the historical obligation to justly interpret and apply the agreements of our predecessors entitles – indeed obliges – us to do what we and those we deal with think is just.

This view of interpretation is reinforced by reflection on the moral purpose which a treaty, as a promise, is supposed to serve. A treaty is supposed to be based on mutual respect, and aims to establish and maintain relations of trust and terms of co-operation acceptable to all parties. In the real world, to be sure, nations have often been forced to sign treaties and accept terms that they regard as unfair. Indigenous people have often had to negotiate from a position of weakness and accept whatever terms that they could get. But when we criticize these treaties, we have in mind an idea of what it means to make a morally acceptable agreement. The Vienna Convention regards as illegitimate treaties that are concluded by coercion or fraud.[24] It is the moral idea of what constitutes a fair agreement that should guide our thinking about what our successors ought to do. Above all, we should want our successors to maintain arrangements that all parties can continue to respect and regard as acceptable. They ought to interpret and apply treaties, change or re-negotiate them, in a way that will maintain respect, trust and mutually accepted terms of co-operation. By making this demand, we commit ourselves to taking the same approach to the agreements made by our predecessors. It is an approach that allows that an agreement is something that evolves, changes its meaning, comes to an end, or is reborn, as the relations between communities develop, and conditions and ideas of acceptability change.

This approach enables us to overcome, at least in principle, a common difficulty that affects the interpretation of many treaties made with indigenous people. The Treaty of Waitangi existed in two main versions, one signed by the representative of the British Crown and one translated into the Maori language and signed by Maori chiefs. The two versions are significantly different. Those responsible for translating the treaty had only a rudimentary understanding of Maori culture and the meanings of key Maori words, and Maoris undoubtedly had only an imperfect understanding of British ideas of sovereignty or what it meant to be a British subject.[25] If a treaty must be interpreted according to the intentions or understandings of its signatories, then there can be no agreed interpretation of the Treaty of Waitangi. But lack of agreement about its original meaning does not prevent Maori and Pakeha from trying to reach an understanding about how it should now be interpreted in the light of present circumstances and views about justice.

Historical injustice

This chapter explains how we acquire obligations that are historical. However, my defence of historical obligations is far from complete. The British Crown made a treaty with Maori chiefs at Waitangi, but the government appointed by the Crown soon broke it. The critical issue for Pakeha New Zealanders, and for the people of nations with similar histories, is not why they should continue to honour a treaty that was made long ago, but what, if anything, they owe to indigenous communities in reparation for violations of historical agreements.

Treaty violations were not the only injustices committed in the past. Across the Tasman Sea from New Zealand, in the Crown Colonies of Australia, governments persistently refused to make agreements of any kind with Aboriginal communities. Appealing to the fiction of 'terra nullius' – the idea that the country was empty of people and available for settlement – governments appropriated the land and opened it to pastoralists, farmers and prospectors. Aborigines were pushed out of the land that their people had occupied for thousands of years, and when they resisted, they were punished. None of these actions violated a treaty, but they clearly count as injustices. The fact that no treaties were made seems itself an injustice. In the United States, Canada, Australia and many other countries, past governments have undermined the culture of indigenous people and destroyed their communities. They have taken away their children and forced them to sell their communal land. A theory of historical obligations has to be able to encompass the demands that these injustices give rise to, not just demands for reparation for broken treaties.

2

Historical Injustice and Respect for Nations

Historical obligations exist. We have an obligation to keep the commitments made by our national predecessors, just as our successors will be obliged to keep those made by us. But nothing so far has been said about reparation for historical injustices. Do we have an obligation to make reparation for the treaty violations of our predecessors? What about other forms of injustice? These questions, I will argue, can be answered by attending to the implications and presuppositions of the practice of transgenerational commitment making. I will begin by explaining why members of nations have a responsibility for making reparations for the treaty violations of their predecessors. Understanding why they have this obligation will provide the key to understanding why they are also responsible for making reparations for injustices that were not violations of treaties – like those committed against Australian Aborigines.

Responsibility for past treaty violations

Political societies have an obligation to keep their promises. This principle, so basic to the relations of nations, depends on members passing down responsibility for keeping a commitment from one generation to another. Treaties are made possible by this transgenerational moral practice. Most people agree with the principle and accept the practice. There is far less agreement about what responsibilities they should bear for past treaty violations committed by leaders or officials of their nation. Widespread resistance to demands for reparation suggests that the first question that has to be answered is not what recompense should be offered to the nation that suffered the violation, but why we should think that anything is owed at all.

Reparative demands for treaty violations are not confined to members of indigenous nations. But the fact that treaties made with indigenous people were so often violated and are now the focus of reparative claims makes these cases of particular interest. The treatment meted out to the Maoris and the Cherokees was the rule, not the exception. In many cases, there never was any intention that agreements made with indigenous communities would be kept. From the start, governments failed to act in the good faith that is morally required of promise makers. Since legitimate excuses for non-performance or bad faith did not exist in the case of most (if not all) of these violations, we have to count them as injustices. Are those who admit that this is so but reject claims for reparation guilty of a moral inconsistency?

Keeping an agreement made by our predecessors forces us to bear burdens that we had no say in incurring. Reparation for historical injustices requires us to make recompense for wrongs which we were in no way responsible for committing. The second demand generates more resistance perhaps, as I suggested earlier, because it is seen as visiting the sins of forebears on their children, as something similar to, and almost as objectionable as, punishing people for crimes they did not commit. This way of perceiving the matter seems to gain some support from the way of arguing that I adopted in the first chapter. Morally responsible citizens will keep the agreements they make, or at least take it upon themselves to repair their unjust violations. But it would not be legitimate for us to break our agreements, enjoy the benefits of injustice, and then require our successors to make recompense for our wrongs. If we did make this demand, then would they not be justified in refusing to fulfil it? So why aren't we also justified in refusing to mop up the moral mess created by our predecessors?

Two intuitively plausible answers to this question, though themselves inadequate, point us in the right direction. We have, first of all, pragmatic reasons for repairing the violations of our predecessors. We continue to coexist with the nations that they mistreated. We want to establish and maintain good relations with members of these nations from now on and into the future. But these people will understandably be reluctant to believe that they are dealing with a nation that can be trusted. We have a better chance of assuring them that our nation takes its commitments seriously if we meet some of their reparative demands. The fact that our irresponsible predecessors left us with this burden is unfortunate and unfair – but our desire to show that our nation is worthy of trust should override our feelings of resentment.

The problem is that this reason for meeting the demands of indigenous peoples does not establish that we are *morally* required to make reparation for the violations of the past – that it can be demanded of us as a matter of justice. Pragmatically motivated actions, as I have suggested, might even fail to achieve their objective. What the recipients want is justice – not simply a gesture designed to placate, which could be made by people who do not really believe that they are obligated to make recompense.

The second answer *does* give us a moral reason for accepting an obligation of reparation – one derived from a reflection on our own failings. Any thoughtful person recognizes that he or she is capable of committing injustice – indeed, is likely to do so. We might do wrong inadvertently, because we hold false beliefs about the behaviour of others or are affected by common prejudices that we have never thought to criticize. Or we might lapse from what we know to be right and become corrupted by greed or some other vice, or we might be forced to do wrong by circumstances beyond our control. It is even more likely that the nation for which we are jointly responsible will commit injustices. But this means that citizens, however morally responsible, know that they are likely to leave unfinished moral business for succeeding generations. We know that we may do injustices that we are unable to repair. We would like our successors to make appropriate recompense if this happens. Perhaps we think that our successors *ought* to do so. But this means that we should be prepared to do the same for our predecessors – at least if we believe that they too were mostly well-meaning people who acted sometimes out of prejudice and believed things that we now know were false.[1]

The idea of a nation as an intergenerational association of (largely) well-meaning people who accept as one of their obligations repairing the moral damage done by their predecessors is appealing and may be motivating. The problem with this way of justifying reparative responsibilities is that it assumes that each generation behaves responsibly. We have (at most) an obligation to repair the violations of our predecessors if we think that they were basically upright people who made mistakes or were in the grip of the prejudices of the times, but not if we think that they were wicked or irresponsible. But some of the worst injustices have been perpetrated by people who should have known better or whose moral behaviour was consistently bad. In any case, there is a lack of fit between this way of reasoning about past injustices and the argument offered in the last chapter for why we should keep the agreements of our predecessors. The latter responsibility does not depend on the intentions of those who made the agreements. So why should our responsibility for making reparation for treaty violations depend on the character or state of mind of the violators?

Fortunately, there is an obvious way of establishing that we have obligations in respect to the violations of our predecessors – one that allows, indeed insists, that they are duties of reparative justice. The moral practice of making posterity-binding commitments brings with it a set of moral requirements. One of these is the obligation to make reparation for violations of commitments. Accepting this responsibility is intrinsic to the practice of making agreements – and not merely something that promotes their acceptance.

When you make an agreement and fail to keep it without having an adequate excuse, then you must accept a responsibility for reparation. Those with whom you have made the agreement have a claim on you. Deceitful people acknowledge their responsibilities, but fail to fulfil them. They are acting in bad faith. But refusing to recognize that a reparative obligation exists does not merely make agents immoral. It removes them from the practice of commitment making altogether. If you make a commitment but deny reparative obligations for failing to honour it, you are not merely acting in bad faith; you are undermining your entitlement to make the commitment. When commitments are posterity-binding, the practice associated with them requires that all the obligations they entail be accepted by the successors of the people who made them. Transgenerational commitments create transgenerational obligations. The practice of making these commitments thus requires our successors to make recompense for violations – including our violations – of our posterity-binding commitments should such violations occur. And we have a corresponding duty to make recompense for the violations of our predecessors.

We get the same result when we put ourselves in the position of those whose trust was violated. When we make an agreement, we have a right to suppose that the others can be trusted to keep it. Being able to have this trust is basic to commitment making. If they do not keep the agreement and have no acceptable excuse, we assume that they have an obligation to make reparation. If we come to believe that we are dealing with people who do not accept this obligation, then we would not regard them as a party with whom commitments can be made. The basis for trust would not exist.

Since agreements persist from one generation to another, so too do reparative entitlements and obligations. It might be objected that the persistence of obligation puts us at the mercy of our forebears. They can commit injustices and leave us to make amends, and there is nothing whatsoever that we can do about it. But at the same time we have them at our mercy. We can thwart their attempts to establish lasting and co-operative relations with other nations. We can destroy their best efforts to be just. If the people of each generation aim only at doing what is in their own interests, if they do not care about the problems they are causing for their successors and refuse to accept responsibility for the injustices of their predecessors, then transgenerational commitments cannot exist. Their existence depends on the willingness of each generation to participate in the practice of honouring commitments and fulfilling the requirements that commitment making entails. This is why we want to assume that our national predecessors were basically well-meaning (though we aren't able to think that all of their commitments were made in good faith). So long as we want to make or maintain transgenerational commitments, we have good reason to value and try to maintain institutions and attitudes that perpetuate the practice of honouring agreements and making amends for failures to do so.

My argument for the persistence of reparative obligations draws on the assumptions that people normally make when they enter into commitments: on beliefs most of us share concerning the implications of commitment making. But transgenerational agreement making, it might be protested, is not a normal case, and it is less clear what making such commitments entails. Why should we not suppose that we are committing our successors to repair only their own violations, leaving us to repair only ours? This question raises a more general difficulty. How do we determine what belongs to the practice of making transgenerational commitments? What do we appeal to if there is a disagreement about this matter?

That we have an obligation to repair the injustices of our predecessors, as well as our own, follows from a consideration of what is owed to those to whom commitments are made. Looking at the matter from their point of view, we have to acknowledge that they are entitled to trust that agreements will be kept. The entitlement to trust is supposed to be passed down through the generations. If the trust is violated, then those who have inherited this entitlement are justified in demanding reparation. The fact that the injustice was done by our predecessors and not by us should not make a difference to the legitimacy of their demand. The business between our communities is not finished; there is an imbalance in our relations that demands repair. This reasoning should suffice to answer the question of why reparative obligations entailed by transgenerational commitments are also transgenerational. More difficult questions about the presuppositions and implications of transgenerational commitment making call for an investigation of the ethical assumptions that lie behind the practice.

Why make commitments?

Why we should engage in the practice of making transgenerational commitments in the first place? Would it be legitimate for a society to avoid such commitments? Answering these questions is not only a necessary step in an argument for the existence of historical obligations. It is also vital in some of the debates concerning injustices committed against nations. British and Australian governments refused to make treaties with Aboriginal communities in Australia. Was their refusal to make agreements itself an injustice? Or was it significant only because it made it easier to commit other injustices against Aborigines?

Those who try to avoid commitment do not always succeed. From a moral point of view, the existence of an agreement between peoples does not depend on the formality of treaty making. The particular ceremonies and legal conventions that have come to surround the making of treaties are not morally important (though they have an obvious legal and political significance). The practice of making agreements should be wide enough to include informal understandings between nations that come into existence through conventions or expectations that each party can be expected to acknowledge. Margaret Gilbert is right to insist that understandings that have the moral force of a joint commitment can come into existence through interactions of certain kinds or by signalling a willingness to enter into a relationship. In the affairs of nations there are some actions that are usually thought to establish such a commitment. For example, if one nation comes to the aid of another – particularly if this aid is solicited – then it is customarily understood that the recipient has a duty of reciprocity should the benefactor be in a similar position of need. The help that the people of East Timor gave to Australians during World War II has been regarded by many Australian citizens as giving their nation a duty to help the East Timorese in their struggle to establish a nation. If a country reduces its stock of weapons, it can be taken in certain circumstances to be signalling a willingness to engage in a mutual process of disarmament. Formal agreements have value because they reduce the possibility of misunderstanding. But formalities are not required in order for commitments and their moral requirements to exist.

So the fact that British and Australian governments did not make formal treaties with Aborigines does not mean that no commitments existed. Governor Philip in the early days of British settlement in Australia declared that Aborigines, as well as settlers, would be protected by law. It would have been reasonable for Aborigines to interpret his statement as an official acknowledgement of their existence and right to fair treatment – indeed, they were meant to so interpret it. Representatives of the colonies frequently negotiated in an informal way with Aborigines, asked for and received their help in exploring the continent – actions that seem to imply recognition and respect for the existence and entitlements of their communities. The subsequent behaviour of governments toward Aborigines – their failure to uphold the law in their defence, or to recognize their communities or their right of possession, can in many cases be regarded as the violation of an understanding, an injustice no less serious from a moral point of view than the violation of a formal treaty.

If transgenerational commitments between nations can come into existence informally through friendly interactions, mutual aid or exchanges of gifts, then the obligations associated with them are difficult to avoid – at least for those nations that live side by side. But avoiding them seems at least possible. Imagine an invading power, arrogant and ruthless, that refuses to have any dealings with native people. It treats them like animals, to be exterminated or pushed aside. Does such a nation by being ruthless and uncooperative avoid the moral consequences of commitment? What is needed is an explanation of why, exactly, such behaviour would be wrong, and thus why agreements between nations are sometimes morally obligatory.

Such an explanation is also needed to fill a gap in the argument of the last chapter. I insisted that we are not relieved from the obligation of keeping the commitments of our predecessors by not making posterity-binding agreements of our own. But this presupposes that we accept the practice of keeping transgenerational commitments. Radical democrats or extreme individualists might consistently refuse to do this. They might argue that no one should be burdened with the responsibility for the acts of past people – neither themselves nor their successors. By adopting this position, they would be eschewing the advantages associated with treaty making. We need to determine whether there is any deeper moral reason for thinking that they are wrong. Finding such a reason is also the first step in an explanation of why citizens can have obligations of reparation for historical injustices other than treaty violations.

Respect for nations

An eighteenth-century British Royal Commission issued the following proclamation on the legal position of the Indian nations of the New World:

The Indians, though living among the king's subjects in these countries, are a separate and distinct people from them, they are treated as such, they have a policy of their own, they make peace and war with any nation of Indians, when they think fit, without control from the English... So that from thence I draw this consequence, that a matter of property in lands in dispute between the Indians as a distinct people and the English subjects, cannot be determined by the law of our land, but by a law equal to both parties, which is the law of nature and nations; and upon this foundation, as I take it, these commissions have most properly issued.[2]

The commission concluded that Indian land was not under the control of the Crown, and that it could only be removed from tribal control through a fair and honest contract – 'a law equal to both parties'.

The law of nature and nations referred to by the commission consists of principles that all reasonable people are supposed to acknowledge – universal requirements of morality that ought to be honoured in law and by political policy makers. By right of this natural law, the commission implies, Indian nations have a status that other nations cannot ignore, a status that requires the British nation, and all other nations, to treat them with respect. What gives Indian nations this status, according to natural law theory, is the fact that they are independent peoples who live according to their own law. This law, by controlling the relations of people within the territory of the nation, also gives a nation rights over its territory. The size of Indian nations, their technology or power in relation to other nations, is irrelevant to the possession of these rights. Respecting Indian nations means recognizing and respecting their status as sovereign peoples and thus their rights of sovereignty. Independent nations cannot be expected to abide by laws determined by others. Their relationship has to be governed by a law made through mutual agreement – by treaties or understandings that all parties can regard as fair. Since the British in the New World could not help but interact with Indian nations, to encroach on their lands, 'the law of nature and nations' required them to reach such understandings and to abide by the agreements they made.

Natural law reasoning tells us that nations that come into contact with each other are morally obliged to make fair agreements concerning the terms of their interaction. From a contemporary perspective, this reasoning is subject to two kinds of objection. Natural law theorists believed that laws governing relations between nations had to be based on moral premises which could lay claim to universality.[3] But the idea that there are universal principles of right that every rational person must acknowledge is now regarded with considerable scepticism. Indigenous Americans probably did not think of their entitlements as 'rights of sovereignty' as Europeans understood them. They had their own way of justifying their entitlement to their land. However, scepticism about universal principles seems to favour the insistence of natural law theorists on the making of agreements between interacting nations that the parties can regard as fair. A nation that governs itself according to its own standards and is capable of making and abiding by its agreements and policies has a claim to respect within a community of law-abiding nations. If we accept the idea that scepticism about moral universals is often thought to promote – that no people is morally entitled to force its laws on another – then we should agree that interactions between nations ought to be governed by mutually acceptable terms of association or co-operation.

Natural law theory picked out as the criterion for being worthy of respect the characteristic that makes it possible for a transgenerational society to make and keep its contracts, to determine and pursue an objective: to be a trustworthy nation among nations. Most contemporary theorists deny that satisfying the condition of being a society governed by a law of its own making is enough to make a nation worthy of respect. The laws of a land can be tyrannical; they can systematically discriminate against particular groups; they can allow atrocities. The status of a nation, according to modern ways of thinking, also depends on the relation between members of a society and its laws, institutions and government. For example, in his explanation of why aggression is the crime of international society, Michael Walzer suggests that states are entitled to have their territory and vital interests respected by others if their authority rests on the consent of their citizens.[4] He is concerned, it is true, with the relation between states in a world of states, but there seems to be no reason why his criterion of respectability could not be applied to semi-independent political societies – collectives describable as 'nations'. Within the limits of their authority, these nations are in many cases ruled by the consent of their members.

The right to respect, Walzer claims, does not stem from a particular form of government. The moral standing of a state (or nation) depends on the reality of the 'common life' it protects, and he thinks that most states do protect the common life of their people. How we should understand his criterion is a matter for debate. Some critics are likely to insist that no non-democratic government can claim to have the consent of those it governs. An account of what the politics of a nation must be like in order to satisfy Walzer's criterion of respectability has to find a balance between the idea that members of a nation should be able to live by their own law – the assumption embodied in the notion of a 'common life' – and the insistence that there are universal moral and political requirements that all political societies must fulfil in order to be worthy of respect. Finding this balance is a difficult undertaking, and I will not attempt it. Fortunately, it is not so difficult to judge that particular nations do satisfy Walzer's criterion. Their governments do not persecute minorities or commit atrocities. Most of their members do accept the authority of their institutions, though they may dislike some of the actions of their leaders.

Two conditions for a state or nation to be considered worthy of respect emerge from this discussion. It must, first of all, be able and willing to respect the integrity and basic interests of other nations and, in particular, be able and willing to keep its commitments, including its transgenerational commitments. Second, its institutions must make and administer the law with an authority derived in some sense from consent of its members. At the very least, it must protect their basic rights. Nations entitled to respect ought to be treated by each other with respect. Being treated with respect, as the Royal Commissioners insisted, means that nations that come into contact with each other, live in proximity with each other, or wish to establish relations of co-operation ought to govern their interactions with an agreement, formal or informal, tacit or explicit, that each can regard as fair. Since nations, and often relations between them, are transgenerational, so too should be at least some of these agreements.

Several consequences follow from these requirements. First of all, members of a nation cannot maintain a principled refusal to make commitments, or even a refusal to make transgenerational agreements. Whenever circumstances put nations into situations that demand negotiation and agreement, refusing to enter into negotiations or to make agreements is an injustice – an act that demonstrates disrespect for an agent that deserves respect. Since it seems reasonable to suppose that Aboriginal nations satisfied the conditions for being respected, it was wrong for British and Australian governments to refuse to make agreements with them. Second, commitments must be made, applied and interpreted in a way compatible with mutual respect. Since nations deserve respect as agents entitled to make the law in their territory and as having responsibility for protecting their members and maintaining their common life, an agreement does not count as fair unless it respects these basic interests, and interpretation of agreements should be compatible with respect. This consequence provides support for the view regarding the interpretation of treaties that I presented in the last chapter.

Reparation and respect

Injustices done to nations include violations other than treaty breaking. The failure to make an agreement when circumstances demand it is such a wrong; so is forcing a nation to make an unfair agreement. Invading and occupying without permission the territory of another nation, or committing in another way what Walzer calls the 'crime of aggression', is an injustice, and so are actions and policies designed to disrupt or destroy the common life of a nation, to undermine its political institutions or the ability of its members to live according to their law. All these injustices are in one way or another acts of disrespect. They either involve a refusal to recognize the authority of the nation's institutions, and the will of the people that lies behind this authority, or they interfere with the ability of people to carry out their responsibilities as members of nations. The question remains whether members of nations have a historical obligation to make reparation for such injustices.

The answer depends on the close relation between commitment making and mutual respect. Those who make commitments are supposed to respect each other and be worthy of respect. The requirement of respect (implicit in the idea of 'good faith') governs how we understand our commitments and how we interpret them. When we as members of a nation make an agreement, formal or informal, with another nation, we commit ourselves and our successors to respect for the legitimate interests of the other party – at least so far as they are relevant to the agreement. What we think that our successors ought to do is not merely keep the terms of our agreements. Indeed, these terms may have to be reinterpreted or even re-negotiated if conditions change. The commitment we are imposing on ourselves and our successors is, above all, a commitment to maintaining relations of respect. Implied by this commitment is the obligation to make reparation for any unjustified act of disrespect. Just as promises carry with them the obligation to make reparation for unjustified breaches, so too do commitments to maintain relations of respect.

By appreciating the presuppositions of promising, we can understand how it is that members of nations can have an obligation to make reparation for acts of disrespect committed by their predecessors – including acts that do not count as violations of a treaty. We can also understand why this obligation exists if we take the perspective of those whom members of our nation have treated with disrespect in the past. These people have to be justified in believing that our successors, as well as ourselves, will respect their integrity and interests. They can reasonably demand that we acknowledge and make recompense for past wrongs in order to demonstrate in a satisfactory way that our nation is now prepared to fulfil the requirements of commitment making – that it is prepared to maintain relations of respect.

This demand is no different from what is often required of individuals. If I have shown little respect for you in the past, you are not likely to regard me as a person with whom you can make a morally binding agreement unless I acknowledge and make recompense for my past injustices. Making reparation is not a pragmatic gesture aimed at achieving a desired result. Acts of injustice, as Boxill says, morally require a response that enables perpetrators and victims to re-establish relations of respect. In the case of relations between nations, responsibilities for reparation, as well as for the keeping of commitments, are transgenerational. In binding our successors to maintain the respectful relations with other nations that underlie transgenerational agreements, we also require them to make reparation for past acts of disrespect, where this is necessary to maintain or re-establish these relations.

This account of our obligations allows that it may not always be *necessary* to make reparation for past wrongs in order to establish or re-establish relations of respect. Suppose I wronged you long ago and have never actually apologized or officially made reparation, yet in more recent times have demonstrated in all kinds of ways that I respect your integrity and interests. You might be able to take my recent actions as an appropriate, if tacit, response to past wrongs, or at least as a reason for believing that we can establish our relationship on a new basis. In later chapters I will argue that the existence of a reparative obligation depends not simply on the fact that our predecessors did a wrong, but also on what has happened between the time of the injustice and the present. Nevertheless, I have established that we can have reparative responsibilities for the injustices of our predecessors – not only for those injustices that involve treaty violations, but also for other acts of disrespect.

Advantages of the theory

The argument for the existence of historical obligations and entitlements involves both forward- and backward-looking considerations. It insists that we have an obligation to keep commitments of the past and to make reparation for past injustices; but it derives the justification for this practice from the moral requirement that members of nations should aim to establish and maintain, now and into the future, respectful relations with other nations.

One of the questions that motivates this study has been answered – at least in general terms. My account of why historical obligations and entitlements exist has some obvious advantages. It does not rest content with an insistence that citizens have these obligations simply because they are citizens. It reveals the moral mechanisms behind treaty keeping and related 'duties of state', and thus provides an explanation of why responsible citizens should accept the sacrifices that these duties entail. My account does not require us to think that we have a duty to the dead or a duty to fulfil the intentions of our predecessors. It thus avoids the problems associated with the intentions of past people and the difficulty of believing that our actions harm or benefit the dead.

It does not tell people that they ought to feel guilt or shame for what their political predecessors did – though it does not claim that such feelings would be irrational. More important, it does not make responsibility depend on ancestry. To have a historical obligation, it is not necessary that you be a descendant of someone who made or violated an agreement. Nor does having an ancestor who fought against the injustice make you exempt. Blood lines are as irrelevant to historical obligations of citizens as they are to other duties of citizenship. You assume the responsibility when you become a citizen – however that occurs. This means that my account is not subject to the common objection that new citizens of a nation, or citizens whose ancestors played no role in committing injustices, cannot be assigned reparative responsibilities for unjust deeds in their nation's past. Recent immigrants or descendants of the guiltless may not be inclined to feel guilt or shame for such misdeeds – people are probably more likely to feel shame or guilt for the unjust deeds of those they count as their ancestors. But this has nothing to do with their responsibilities as citizens.[5]

My account not only rejects the commonly held view that responsibility for the past runs in families or ethnic blood lines. It rejects family or kinship relations as a basis for historical obligation. Responsibilities with respect to deeds of the past belong only to associations capable of making and keeping transgenerational commitments. Families, at least in modern Western societies, cannot make such commitments. A father cannot reasonably demand that his children keep his promises or make reparation for the wrongs he has done, and if he does make this demand, his children will regard it as within their rights to refuse to fulfil it.[6] A kinship or ethnic group is a collection of people who share certain characteristics and cultural values or have a common relationship. It is not an association capable of making and keeping transgenerational commitments. Nations, it is true, are not the only associations that have this capacity. Corporations, churches and other such collectivities can generally satisfy the conditions, and what I have said about the historical obligations of nations in these two chapters will also apply to them.

Finally, the account I have given makes a less obvious, but equally important, contribution to discussions about justice in a political society. It brings to prominence something that is ignored or marginalized in most theories of justice: the moral relationship between the generations. Maintaining a political society capable of acting justly in a world of nations depends essentially on a moral practice that requires each generation of citizens to take responsibility for keeping the commitments of its predecessors and repairing their injustices. Our transgenerational responsibilities, I will argue in later chapters, extend beyond relations with other nations.

Establishing that we have historical obligations is a significant step, but it is obvious that a theory about historical obligations and entitlements, even the part of it that concentrates on relations between nations, requires much more. What citizens need to know is not merely that they have an obligation to make recompense for historical injustices committed by leaders or officials of their nation, but what exactly this obligation requires them to do, and how reparative obligations are related to duties of other kinds. The first step toward answering these questions is to take a closer look at the nature of reparative justice: what a theory of reparative justice should aim to accomplish and the perspective it should adopt.

3

Theories of Reparation

Reparation is customarily assigned a place in a tripartite scheme that distinguishes the forms that justice takes in legal systems and moral theories. 'Positive justice' consists of rights and duties that belong to individuals or groups and the entitlements or obligations that they acquire through contracts, treaties or other historical acts. Retributive justice is concerned with punishment of offenders for violations of requirements of positive justice, so far as these are embodied in law; reparative justice with restitution or recompense for violations. Retributive and reparative justice, says W. D. Lamont, *'maintain* the system which [positive] justice has *created'*.[1] Since positive justice plays the primary role in this scheme, most philosophical energy has been put into the development or criticism of principles of justice or theories of rights.[2] Retributive justice has received less attention, and reparative justice scarcely any at all.

One reason for the lack of attention to reparative justice is that its requirements and purpose seem straightforward and uncontroversial.[3] People argue about principles of positive justice; they disagree about whether the purpose of a system of punishment is to punish wrongdoers according to the seriousness of their crime, or whether it should be designed to serve social ends like deterrence or protection of society. But those who pay attention to reparative justice seem to assume that no serious disagreements about matters of principle or purpose are likely to take place in its territory. Two assumptions are usually taken to be self-evident: that if a person's (or community's) rights are violated, or his or her interests unjustly harmed, then reparative justice demands that the injustice be remedied; and that reparative justice has been achieved if and only if the victim is returned to the position that he or she was in before the injustice was done, or obtains compensation equivalent in value to what was lost through the injustice.[4] These propositions outline a rights-centred, restorative approach to reparative justice. In this chapter I will argue against both. In doing so, I will show that there are alternative views about the scope and objective of reparative justice. A theory of reparation can be 'rights-centred' or 'obligations-dependent'; it can aim to achieve restoration or reconciliation. I will provide reasons for adopting an obligations-dependent, reconciliatory approach.

Rights and obligations

A rights-centred theory of reparation focuses on the rights or interests of individuals and communities, and insists that any violation of these rights or any unjustified harm to these interests calls for reparation. Once it has been established that a violation has occurred, there is no doubt about the existence of a reparative obligation. An obligations-dependent theory, on the other hand, holds that the right to reparation for an injustice depends on the existence of an agent or agents with the obligation to make reparation for the wrong, and that the only agents who can be assigned this obligation are those responsible for the injustice or, in the case of the actions of an organized group like a nation, the successors of those responsible. For an obligations-dependent theory, the fact that an unjustified harm has occurred is not sufficient reason for believing that reparation is due.

In the last two chapters I have adopted an obligations-dependent approach. I have assumed that the question 'Do historical obligations for reparation exist?' has to be answered, and have argued that the existence of these obligations does not follow simply from the fact that rights have been violated or even that some individuals have benefited from historical injustices and others have suffered harm. I have assumed that a right to reparation for a historical injustice depends on establishing that the successors of the perpetrators have an obligation to make reparation. In the case of historical injustices, the obligations approach seems the natural one to take. Members of nations who are not themselves responsible for an injustice *do* often question whether they have a responsibility for reparation (and if they do not, then presumably no one does). They are not doubting that their predecessors committed injustices or that presently existing people suffer harm because of these injustices. They doubt that the requirements of reparative justice are applicable to them. What is more, an obligations-dependent approach can provide a plausible reason as to why we think that some reparative claims would be absurd. The Greek government does not owe reparations to the descendants of Athenian helots. What stands in the way of a reparative claim is not merely that these descendants cannot be identified. The Athenian state no longer exists, and it is not reasonable to suppose that the modern Greek state has inherited any of its responsibilities. No existing community has reparative responsibilities for the depredations of the ancient Greeks and Romans, and therefore no one can claim reparation for the injustices they committed. The rights approach has a more difficult time explaining why violations of rights that took place long ago – particularly violations of right of possession – cease to be the legitimate focus of reparative claims.

An obligations-dependent approach gains plausibility from the way it treats cases of historical injustice – but this does not mean that it is right. It needs a more systematic defence. I will argue that a rights-centred approach has counter-intuitive implications that an obligations-dependent approach can more easily escape.

Compensation and reparative justice

An attractive feature of the rights-centred approach is that it concentrates on the situation and suffering of the victim. His rights have been violated; his interests have been harmed unjustly. If someone is not made responsible for reparation, then an injustice will fail to be remedied. Nevertheless, the emphasis placed by the rights-centred approach on undoing the harm caused by an injustice tends to collapse useful and intuitively plausible distinctions between reparative and remedial justice, and between reparation and compensation for unjustified inequality. The versatile term 'compensation' makes it especially easy to ignore these distinctions.

Nozick, as already mentioned, holds that rectification is due for any violation of rights, whether caused by deliberate wrongdoing or by an accidental or excusable action. Indeed, there is no reason why entitlement to rectification, from a rights-centred point of view, should depend on there being any agent to whom the wrong can be attributed. An unjustified harm could be brought about as the result of the actions of many agents none of whom intend or even foresee the unfortunate result. According to many theories of positive justice, unjustified harm can be caused by a natural disaster or a genetic fault. If almost all of the water-holes in a desert community dry up, those members deprived of this essential resource are unjustifiably harmed. If a person is born blind, then, according to some positive theories of justice, she is unjustly disadvantaged; she is suffering from a harm that requires compensation. According to its own logic, the rights-centred approach will find it difficult to resist endorsing an entitlement to rectification or compensation to all those who are unjustly disadvantaged, however that injustice was caused. Reparation, so conceived, is simply compensation for unjustified disadvantage, and reparative justice covers the whole field of remedial justice (as the tripartite scheme mentioned in the first paragraph assumes).[5]

However, this result is counter-intuitive. We do not regard every kind of compensation for injustice as reparation. Boxill is following a more customary way of thinking of the matter when he insists that reparation is different from compensation for unjustified disadvantage. Without this distinction, there is no way of making claims that people often want to make. For example, those who think that there is a case for black reparations want to distinguish the reparative demands that they think American blacks can make because of slavery and other historical injustices from the demands they can make on the ground of equity – because their existing needs have not been met or because they suffer from disadvantages relative to the white population of the USA. An unjustified inequality, however caused, ought to be remedied. This is a duty entailed by the acceptance by members of a society of particular principles of justice. But a reparative claim, as we usually understand it, is addressed to those who were responsible for the injustice (or their successors), and on them falls the obligation of reparation.

The violation of a right, according to the rights-centred approach, brings into being an obligation of reparation (or rectification); but the approach is not specific about who should bear the burden so long as the responsibility is not unjustly assigned. This lack of specificity can also have counter-intuitive consequences. Suppose that in our village an injustice has been done by the members of one clan to those of another. The demands of the victims for reparation go unheeded until the rich man of the village, who does not belong to either clan, averts a protracted dispute by volunteering to compensate the victims for what they lost through the injustice. The victims have received a remedy for their suffering, but they have not obtained reparation, according to most people's understanding of what this means. The distinction between rights-centred and obligations-dependent ideas of reparation also allows us to distinguish between the compensation that some governments provide to victims of crime and the arrangement, advocated by some legal theorists, that would require criminals to make reparations to their victims.[6]

Reparation, according to the obligations-dependent approach, is owed only by the agent – individual or community – responsible for the injustice. Its emphasis on establishing responsibility allows it to make distinctions that a rights-centred theory ignores or downplays. It distinguishes between remedial responses to injustice (which can result from the good will or sense of justice of a third party) and reparation owed by the agent responsible for the injustice. It removes from the sphere of reparative justice remedies for unjust inequalities that cannot be blamed on agents: inequalities that are the result of the interactions of blameless agents, or those that stem from natural disasters or genetic factors. These inequalities, according to some theories of positive justice, are unjust and should be remedied, but their remedy is not the business of a theory of reparation. Obligations-dependent reparation has no difficulty making a distinction between a community's duty to remedy those unjustified disadvantages which fall within its sphere of responsibility and agents making reparation for the rights they violated. For an obligations-dependent approach, reparative justice is not the same as remedial justice, and the duty of people of a society to remove unjust disadvantages cannot be conflated with the obligation of an agent to repair the wrong he or she has done. Accepting an obligations-dependent theory requires revision of the tripartite scheme mentioned at the beginning of this chapter.

The fact that an obligations-dependent approach is conducive to making intuitively plausible distinctions amounts to a good case for it. But something must be said about the intuitions which support the rights-centred approach. Those who take an obligations-dependent approach have to admit that some injustices will remain forever unrequited simply because the agents who committed them no longer exist or cannot make reparation. This means that there will be no *reparation* for harms and losses caused by these injustices – though not necessarily no *remedy*. This consequence of the approach not only seems unfair; in some circumstances it seems to result in absurdity. If a thief dies shortly after the theft, does this mean that the victim can make no claim for reparation? Moreover, accepting an obligations-dependent approach means that many claims that victims or their descendants want to make cannot be justified by a theory of reparation. A nation cannot claim a territory in reparation for unjust dispossession if the agent which committed the wrong has ceased to exist (and there is no successor to which the responsibility can be reasonably assigned). An obligations-dependent view of reparation would not have given Zionists an entitlement to claim the land of Israel even though this land was once Hebrew territory from which

Jews were unjustly expelled. It cannot give indigenous people the right to lay claim to the land of their ancestors *just because* this territory was unjustly taken from their nation. Some people may find such consequences of the obligations-dependent approach uncongenial or at least counter-intuitive. But, worst of all, it seems that an obligations-dependent approach prevents descendants of victims of injustice from making legitimate reparative claims. Slave owners have long ago departed from the scene. How, then, can black Americans make a legitimate demand for reparation for slavery?

Some of these objections are easily answered. Slave owners are dead, and many of the injustices done to slaves are indeed beyond the scope of reparative justice. But the nation which for a long time tolerated slavery and failed to make reparations to former slaves is still in existence. Allowing an injustice to take place when a community has the power to prevent it, failing to remedy injustice or to make reparation when it is owed, are themselves injustices for which reparation can be demanded. In other words, sufficient wrong can be attributed to the American nation to give descendants of slaves a case for reparation (though whether their claims can be justified remains to be seen). The responsibilities of citizens for repairing the injustices of their nation do not depend (as I argued earlier) on their participation in this wrongdoing, or even on their being descendants of those who did the wrong.

If a thief dies shortly after his theft, we would naturally suppose that reparation ought to be made from his estate, which can be reasonably regarded as an extension of himself. If he has been dead for a longer time, then reparations can be extracted from members of his family if they were accessories to his life of crime (or if we can claim that they should have known that their possessions were derived from criminal activity). But if they and others who have made use of the stolen goods were completely innocent, then they do not owe reparation, according to the obligations-dependent view. These results seem to accord fairly well with our intuitions about when people have been unjustly enriched and when this accusation is difficult to sustain.

This defence of an obligations-dependent approach is not going to satisfy everyone. Some philosophers – Nozick is a notable example – believe that having a historical title to their possessions gives individuals an unconditional right to reparation when the rights given to them by this title are violated. The right of rectification, they believe, should not depend on the presence of the agents responsible for the violation. A defence of an obligations-dependent approach against this view awaits a critical examination of the notion of 'historical title', which I will leave for the next chapter.

Responsibility

Reparative obligations, according to the obligations-dependent approach, fall only on agents – on individuals or collectives responsible for the injustice. Those who take an obligations-dependent approach must therefore provide some account of when agents are responsible for injustice. There are two contending theories. According to the first, agents are responsible for an injustice if and only if they are culpable: when and only when they deliberately commit wrongs, or negligently allow unjustified harm to occur, or fail to prevent wrongs when they have a responsibility to do so and have no good excuse for their failure. The second does not require that an agent be culpable in order to be held responsible for reparation. It is enough that she has violated the rights of another or failed to fulfil a reasonable expectation – even though her action or failure to act might be excusable.

Our intuitions seem to favour the second account. Consider a case presented by Joel Feinberg.

> Suppose that you are on a backpacking trip in the high mountain country when an unanticipated blizzard strikes the area with such ferocity that your life is imperiled. Fortunately, you stumble onto an unoccupied cabin, locked and boarded up for the winter, clearly someone's private property. You smash the window, enter, and huddle in a corner for three days until the storm abates. During this period you help yourself to your unknown benefactor's food supply and burn his wooden furniture in the fireplace to keep warm.[7]

Your actions are justifiable. There is no question of your being liable to punishment. Nevertheless, Feinberg believes that you owe compensation to the property owner for the damage you have done. You have, after all, done him an injury, violated his property rights, even though this harm can be justified as necessary to save your life.[8]

Most people are likely to feel guilty for doing something that harms another, and think that they have a responsibility for repair, even if they couldn't help causing the harm. Richard Swinburne thinks that this is a 'virtually unanimous moral intuition'. 'If I unintentionally break your best vase, or light the fire with the only copy of your book, I acquire the status of a wrongdoer even if my actions were done in total ignorance of their nature or consequences.'[9] At the very least I owe you an apology. Swinburne thinks that responsibility in these cases arises out of an understanding with those with whom I interact that 'I undertake responsibility for seeing that certain things are done and certain things are not done' which my clumsy or unintentional behaviour has flouted.[10]

The difference in focus of retributive and reparative justice supports this idea. Retributive justice is concerned with the offender. We are entitled to punish her simply because she is wicked (as retributionists believe), or because we have a right to protect ourselves from her, to make her mend her ways, or to use her as an example to deter others (as utilitarians think). If she did something unintentionally, or with a good excuse, then she is not wicked; we do not have to protect ourselves from her or reform her, and by punishing her we are not likely to deter others. Reparative justice, on the other hand, is concerned with the victim and the relation between victim and perpetrator. We are entitled to trust the people with whom we interact, and if this trust is violated, however unintentionally, then we are unjustifiably harmed, and the person who violated the trust should take responsibility for repair.

It might be objected that a theory of reparation that demands recompense for unintended harms is in danger of collapsing the distinction made above between acts that require reparation and other harms that ought to be remedied. The uncoordinated actions of people pursuing their separate interests can result in unfair losses for some (as sometimes happens in economic affairs). If lack of intention to harm is no defence against being blameworthy, then why can we not make these agents responsible for reparation? The answer, I believe, is that in cases where harm is the result of the behaviour of uncoordinated agents, there is too much of a gap between the particular actions of individuals and the resulting harm to regard them as blameworthy. No person can know in such circumstances whether her actions contributed to the effect, or which actions did contribute, or to what degree. No one can say that if she had not acted as she did, the harm would not have occurred. This means that she is not likely to regard her actions as violating any understanding between herself and others. And an uncoordinated collection of individuals is not itself an agent, and cannot be blamed for anything. If, for example, the economic activities of a large, indefinite group of people result in high unemployment, then, according to many views about equity, this is a harm which people of a nation ought to remedy. However, there is no reason to think of the remedy as reparation, or for anyone to apologize for the harm (unless the blame can be pinned on the policies of leaders). The actions that produced the result are not like the unintentional breaking of a vase, which was the deed of a particular person, and would not have occurred if he had not dropped it.

The culpability of our predecessors for historical injustices is often hard to doubt. They deliberately broke treaties they had made, invaded and destroyed communities without having, so far as we can tell, a legitimate excuse. But the view we adopt concerning responsibility for reparation will affect our response to cases where culpability is in dispute. The invasion by Europeans of the lands of indigenous people in the Americas, Australia, New Zealand and Africa has often been excused by the following argument.

'Once indigenous nations came within the ambit of European exploration and exploitation, a European invasion was inevitable. Those individuals and nations hungry for gold, land or power were not going to leave indigenous people alone. The only question was which European nations would seize the opportunities. In the competition for colonies, no nation could afford to take the moral high ground. If England had not assumed control over Australia, New Zealand and as much of North America as it could grab, some other nation would have done so – to the detriment of vital British interests.' The argument claims that the agents in this case – nations, individuals and companies – were acting under the force of circumstances – they had little choice but to do what they did, and thus were not culpable for the crime of aggression, any more than the backpacker was culpable for invading the cabin. The issue here is not whether the excuse was ever plausible (and how we could determine this), but whether its plausibility as an excuse matters as far as present reparative responsibilities are concerned.

If we take the position of Feinberg and Swinburne, it does not. Whatever excuses the invaders might have had, the fact remains that their incursions took place, with resulting disasters for indigenous people and their nations. The position I defended in chapters 1 and 2 provides an independent reason for adopting this view. I argued that the intentions of our predecessors are not relevant to whether we have an obligation to keep their commitments. It would be odd, if not a downright inconsistency, if the beliefs and intentions of our predecessors, even if they could be discovered, were relevant to whether we owe reparations for their deeds.

So far I have found reasons for supporting an obligations-dependent approach to reparation, which makes those responsible for doing a wrong (or their successors), whether culpable or not, responsible for reparation for injustices. There are some further decisions to be made about our approach to reparative justice.

Restoration and reconciliation

There are two discourses about responses to wrongdoing. The first is 'legalistic'. It talks about rights and obligations, restoration and compensation. It is the discourse with which the term 'reparation' is most often associated. The second is more 'theological'. It is concerned with apology, forgiveness, contrition, atonement and reconciliation. Neither discourse excludes the other; but what is important to one is marginal or unimportant to the other. Those who adopt the first discourse do not think of apology or the reconciliation of the parties as a requirement of reparation. They are more likely to regard apology or acknowledgement of wrong as an extra courtesy that wrongdoers ought to extend, and reconciliation as a desirable effect that might be achieved by reparation. But apology or expression of regret for the wrong done is central for those who adopt the second discourse. They regard reparation as incomplete or unsatisfactory without it.[11]

Those who adopt the first discourse think that reparation has not been made until the victims have been restored to the position they were in before the injustice was done or have been provided with something equivalent in value. Those who adopt the second think that reparation has been achieved when the parties have been reconciled: when the wrongdoer has apologized and made recompense, and when the victim has forgiven the wrong, or, in cases where forgiveness is not possible, is at least prepared to resume peaceful, co-operative relations. For those who adopt the discourse of reconciliation, reparation can be achieved even when restoration has not, or cannot, be made. Indeed, they insist that restoration by itself is not sufficient to achieve reparation. If the parties remain unreconciled, the process is incomplete.

The first discourse can be described as being about 'reparation as restoration', and the second as being about 'reparation as reconciliation'. Each can be understood as an account of what reparation means. In the internal and external affairs of nations, reparation usually has the meaning of restoration or compensation. But some nations in their response to past wrongdoing have chosen the path of reconciliation. South Africa's attempt through the Truth and Reconciliation Commission to come to terms with wrongs committed during the apartheid era is an obvious example. A reconciliatory theory requires an obligations-dependent approach. Reconciliation makes sense only if there is a wrongdoer able and willing to engage in an act of reconciliation. Those who are not wrongdoers do not need to repair relations. A restorative approach, on the other hand, does not logically entail, nor is it logically entailed by, a rights-centred approach; it is compatible with either. However, rights-centred theories are usually restorative. They generally assume that reparation for a violation of a right restores the victim to the enjoyment of that right.

Both reparation as restoration and reparation as reconciliation are concerned with past injustices, whether historical or more recent, but restorative reparation is 'backward-looking', in that it insists that reparation should restore the victim to his prior position. By contrast, reconciliatory reparation is 'forward-looking', in the sense that it aims to achieve a good outcome now or in the future. In this respect restorative reparation is similar to the retributive theory of punishment, which insists that wrongdoers be punished according to the nature and severity of their crime, and reconciliatory reparation resembles the utilitarian approach to punishment, which holds that punishment should aim to produce good effects for society. However, retributive and utilitarian theories of punishment are well worked-out, independent positions. Restorative and reconciliatory views of reparation are not independent of each other, and neither is adequate by itself.

One difficulty with the objective of restoration is that achieving it is often beyond human powers. Those unjustly killed cannot be brought back to life; property can be returned, but not the opportunities that the victims' children would have had if the injustice had not been done. Gerald Gaus thinks that the problem is even more serious: he argues that reparation as a return to equality – in my terminology, restorative reparation – can *never* be accomplished.[12] If a person has wronged another, then there is no way that this injury can be undone. For a wrong involves the failure to demonstrate proper respect; it is a disruption of the moral order. Perpetrators cannot undo a failure of respect any more than they can undo murder. Restoration merely provides the victim with possessions, money or new opportunities. It doesn't restore the moral balance.

In claiming that reparation cannot restore equality, Gaus is concerned exclusively with harms for which the perpetrator is culpable. Nevertheless, the fact that people feel remorse for the harm they have done even when it was the result of an accident, and often think that they ought to apologize, suggests that even inadvertent wrongs create moral dissonance between victim and wrongdoer that restoration by itself will not bridge. Suppose that an accident-prone magnate visits your house and in the course of his perambulations breaks several of your precious ornaments. He goes away without acknowledging, let alone apologizing, for what he has done, but the next day an agent whom he employs for this purpose comes around and gives you a cheque for the damage caused plus a bit extra for the trouble you have to take to buy new ornaments. You are likely to think that he has treated you disrespectfully, even though restoration has been made.

Gaus thinks that he is showing that the goal of reparation as philosophers have conceived of it since the time of Aristotle cannot be achieved.[13] Reparative justice, he concludes, has to adopt the more modest objective of compensating for the harm done by a wrong to the extent that this is possible. Since he thinks that reparative justice is by its nature restorative (even though its objective cannot be fulfilled), he regards apology, forgiveness, mercy and other attempts to bridge the moral gulf between perpetrators and victims as responses that take place outside the realm of justice.[14] For those disposed to take a reconciliatory view, his argument seems better understood as a criticism of reparation as restoration. The restorative account of what reparation means is inadequate, because it fails to address the harm done by a wrong to relations of respect that ought to obtain between individuals or nations.[15] Acts of disrespect cannot be undone, but they can be acknowledged, apologized for, and sometimes forgiven. Through these responses relations of respect can be re-established. The solution, it seems, is to incorporate these acts into a theory of reparation – to give them a central place. But this move would amount to adopting a theory of reconciliatory reparation, or moving in that direction.

The reasons for rejecting reparation as restoration give us grounds for supporting reconciliatory reparation. Nevertheless, achieving reconciliation cannot be regarded as either a necessary or a sufficient condition for satisfying the demands of reparative justice. It cannot be a necessary condition, because an intransigent victim might make outrageous reparative demands, or adamantly refuse to accept anything that the perpetrator can offer. Surely, a perpetrator who has done all she can to make repair, must have either satisfied the requirements of reparation, or gone some way to satisfying them, even if her victim is completely unreconciled. Nor can reconciliation be a sufficient condition for the achievement of reparative justice. The mere fact that the victims are prepared to live in peace with, or even forgive, the perpetrators does not mean that justice has been done. The victims may have been too eager to forgive, or they may have been forced by the greater power of the perpetrator to accept an

unfair settlement. If we make it a condition of the theory that reconciliation must be just, then we have to give an account of what counts
as a just reconciliation – and this means explaining what reparative
demands can be justified. Is it just for members of an indigenous
nation to demand land unjustly taken from their ancestors? Is it just
for black Americans to demand $500 million (the sum named by
James Forman in the Black Manifesto) in reparation for the enslavement of their ancestors? A theory of reconciliatory reparation, in
other words, cannot avoid questions that are of concern to those
who regard reparation as a matter of restoration.

Reconciliation reconstructed

In responding to the inadequacies of both restorative and reconciliatory theories, we seem to have two choices. We can maintain the
paradoxical position advocated by Gaus and hold on to a restorative
theory while admitting that restoration is not achievable. Alterna-
tively, we can develop the reconciliatory approach by incorporating
into it an idea of a just settlement. We could retain the attractive idea
that the purpose of reparation is reconciliation, but lay down guidelines concerning what the perpetrator is required to do to bring about
a just reconciliation.

   If we take the latter course, then we need a more precise and less
problematic idea of what reconciliation means. Reconciliation cannot
mean in all cases that the offence has been forgiven or that relations
are henceforth harmonious and co-operative. Some wrongs may be
unforgivable (as many people say about the crimes of the Nazis). And
individuals and nations can be divided about other things besides the
injustices in their history. Conflicts of interest may continue to make
their relations strained. But reconciliation without forgiveness seems
possible; and so does reconciliation in which individuals or nations
put behind them resentments that stem from past injustices, even
though they have other reasons for conflict. A better understanding
of reconciliation – one that generalizes from the discussion in the last
chapter – is that reconciliation is achieved when the harm done by
injustice to relations of respect and trust that ought to exist between
individuals or nations has been repaired or compensated for by the
perpetrator in such a way that this harm is no longer regarded as
standing in the way of establishing or re-establishing these relations.
An act or process of reconciliation that accomplishes this objective
counts as a just reconciliation. Victims are not obliged or entitled to
regard reconciliation as just unless their just demands are satisfied,

and so the reference to repair or compensation for harm has to be filled out with an account of what counts as a just demand.

Aiming for reconciliation cannot guarantee success. Attempts can fail because the victims are intransigent, because they have ideas about justice that are different from the ideas of the perpetrators, or because nothing that the perpetrator has the power to do is capable of bringing it about that the harm of the injustice no longer stands in the way of relations of respect. Since nations and individuals should seek to establish and maintain relations of respect, intransigence without an adequate justification is wrong. A theory of reparation as restoration assigns obligations only to perpetrators (or their successors). But a reconciliatory theory holds that victims have an obligation to accept reparation that they have reason to regard as just, and thus to play a morally responsible role in the process of reconciliation.[16] The possibility remains that some injustices may be so serious that the victims cannot accept reparation, whatever form it takes, without damage to their self-respect. But since individuals and nations should seek respectful relations with each other, for the sake of their descendants and successors as well as themselves, they should not be too ready to stand on their dignity. Disagreements about justice are bound to arise whatever theory of reparation we adopt, but (as I will explain below) these disagreements are not likely to be an insurmountable problem in the context of a reconciliatory theory.

One of the obvious advantages of a reconciliatory theory is that it is able to explain how reparation can be made in cases where restoration, or even compensation, is impossible. It explains why symbolic gestures like apologies can count as reparation.[17] They do not restore lives that have been lost or bring it about that suffering did not happen. But by demonstrating a remorseful acknowledgement of a past wrong, they can make it possible for nations or individuals to re-establish relations of respect. When Konrad Adenauer, the chancellor of post-war Germany, offered to pay reparation to Israel for the persecution, slaughter and dispossession of Jews, neither he nor anyone else supposed that any payment could compensate for the harm done. The crimes were beyond repair – well outside the scope of reparation as restoration. Yet it is reasonable to regard his offer as reparation with a reconciliatory purpose. At least part of his intent was to show that Germans acknowledged the seriousness of past wrongs and desired to regain a moral standing in the eyes of the rest of the world, and in particular in the eyes of those who represented the victims. The amount paid was determined by what negotiators on both sides could agree was appropriate in the light of this objective.

Those who enter such negotiations are likely to have different views about what is just. Reconciliation is a process of mutual accommodation that presupposes the acceptance of moral conditions and objectives. Nations and individuals ought to establish relations of respect (except when there is good reason to believe that the other is not worthy of respect, either in a particular context or in general). They ought to aim at reconciliation as I defined it. In their negotiations they ought to treat each other with respect. They ought to seek an agreement that enables them to maintain these respectful relations. These moral requirements, when fulfilled, will predispose parties to reach an agreement that each from their point of view can regard as fair. They will be prepared to appreciate each other's position, accommodate themselves to it, and make compromises. The reconciliatory approach allows for the possibility that parties may have different views about justice and the events of history. Reconciliation is a process involving discourse, in which each attempts to reach what Rawls calls an 'overlapping consensus': a result that each can endorse from his or her point of view.[18]

In reaching this consensus, the parties, to satisfy the moral requirements of reconciliation, will be predisposed to take into account present conditions and needs. Since their aim should be to reach a settlement that enables them to maintain respectful relations, and, if possible, put behind them grievances rooted in the past, they should be prepared to interpret restorative demands or treaty provisions in the light of present realities and needs. Those who make demands will not impose conditions that would threaten the existence or security or undermine the economic well-being of the other. They will be prepared to accommodate the needs of the other. A reconciliatory approach is thus in a position to solve, at least in theory, the problem of relating reparative demands to other requirements of justice.

There is a further reason to adopt a theory that defines reparation as reconciliation. The position I have been arguing for in the last two chapters does not presuppose or entail either a restorative or a reconciliatory theory of reparation. The arguments I have used to explain why members of nations have reparative entitlements and obligations appeal to the requirements and presuppositions of commitment making. They do not tell us what we should do once we acknowledge the existence of these obligations. Nevertheless, by positioning the debate about the existence of historical obligations in the context of ongoing relations between nations, my account provides a reason for finding the reconciliatory approach congenial. If we are morally motivated to accept historical obligations because of a belief that our successors ought to keep our agreements and maintain respectful relations with those nations with whom we interact, then we will be drawn to an approach to reparative entitlements and obligations that focuses on repairing the harm done by injustice to respectful relationships. If we think that the requirements of treaties ought to be interpreted in a way that maintains relations of respect, then it is reasonable to think that in fulfilling our reparative obligations for broken treaties and similar wrongs we should aim to re-establish relations of respect.

These remarks should be enough to establish that a reconciliatory theory provides a defensible and attractive approach to reparation. I will develop it and put it to the test in the following chapters.

4

Land Rights and Reparation

In 1868 the Sioux nation signed a treaty with the United States government at Fort Laramie, Wyoming, which guaranteed protection of their territory in the Black Hills. However, when gold was discovered in the Black Hills, the government found it increasingly inconvenient to protect the entitlements of the Sioux from the prospectors and settlers who flooded into the area, and it put pressure on the leaders of the tribe to sell their land. Though their people were starving, they refused. 'One does not sell the land that people walk in,' said Chief Crazy Horse.[1] The government decided to solve the problem by military means, and though Sioux resistance was ferocious, and for a time effective, the Sioux were finally defeated, removed from the Black Hills, and settled on reservations.

As white settlement in the area increased, Sioux territory was further diminished, and by the beginning of the twentieth century the Sioux had been confined to a small area in the Dakotas. However, the Sioux never gave up the fight for reparation, and over many years pursued claims through the courts which were vigorously opposed at every turn by the US government. In 1980 the Supreme Court finally awarded them a $122 million payment as compensation for 'a ripe and rank case of dishonourable dealing'. But, despite their poverty, the Sioux have so far refused to accept the money. They insist that the Black Hills rightfully belongs to them, and that no settlement is acceptable that does not include its return.

The money offered by the Supreme Court was probably inadequate compensation for the loss of their territory and other injustices. But this is not the main issue for the Sioux. They are not asking for more money. They regard their demand for their ancestral land as basic and non-negotiable. The critical question raised by this case is whether this demand is justified. Are the Sioux right to believe that return of the Black Hills is the only just reparation for injustices committed against them? A theory of reparation, whatever form it takes, has to be able to answer questions like these.

To justify their claim, the Sioux often appeal to the treaty that guaranteed their possession of the Black Hills. The existence of this treaty played an important role in the decision made by the court. But from a moral point of view, treaties are not sufficient to justify land claims. We can agree that broken promises require reparation, yet regard as an open question the form that reparation should take. Giving back what was taken may have been the right thing to do at one time, but not any more. How we should interpret a treaty and what we should do about broken treaties, says Robert E. Goodin, depend on what is fair in the present day.[2] The Supreme Court was of the opinion that monetary compensation was fair. To defend the claim of the Sioux, we have to appeal to something more morally basic than the terms of a treaty.

Some philosophers believe that the justification of the claim made by the Sioux, and by others who claim the land of their ancestors, rests on the existence of a historical title. They understand the Sioux to be asserting a right of possession over the Black Hills, a right that existed prior to the treaty and which the treaty was supposed to protect. The Sioux are entitled to the land of their ancestors, according to this view, because it continues to belong to them. Their right of possession was never voluntarily surrendered; so those who now inhabit the Black Hills have no right to it. This defence of the Sioux claim takes a rights-centred, restorative approach to reparation. A claim that rests on historical title is thus a challenge to the obligations-dependent reconciliatory approach to reparative justice advocated in the last chapter.

In this chapter I will defend the land claim of the Sioux and, by implication, many of the land claims made by indigenous nations. However, I will argue that the best defence rests not on an appeal to historical title, but on a consideration of what reparation is appropriate in the light of a history of injustice. The case for reparation that I will be arguing is not only compatible with a reconciliatory (and thus an obligations-dependent) approach. It is best understood in that framework.

Historical title

A historical title to land or some other possession is a right arising from a historical act, relationship or process. It belongs to an individual (or a community) because of acts that he or she (or it) performed or because of the acts of particular others, and not because of someone's status as a human being or member of a community. A historical title, so understood, is morally basic. It is supposed to give individuals or communities an entitlement independent of law, social conventions or treaties to possess and use particular things or resources. Since it is an entitlement that laws and treaties are supposed to recognize and protect, it seems that the best moral defence of Sioux demands would appeal to their historical title over the Black Hills. But this defence must explain why such a title existed, and why it continues to persist long after the Sioux have been separated from the land of their ancestors.

Most theories that attempt to justify historical title take as their point of reference John Locke's theory of 'original appropriation'. Locke thinks of natural resources as originally belonging to all humankind, and thus has to explain how individuals or groups can justify excising a portion of this common stock and treating it as their own. He thinks that private appropriation is justified by labour: by people cultivating a piece of land or engaging in other acts of production and improvement ('mixing labour with a thing', as he puts it).[3] Having through their labour acquired property, these individuals or groups have the moral right to use it, exclude others, sell it or give it away. Locke's theory, so often used by settlers and governments as a justification for expropriating the land of indigenous people, seems an unpromising basis for an attempt to ground the land rights of an indigenous community. A better understanding of indigenous cultures and economies, or a more generous interpretation of 'cultivation', might enable us to refute the common notion (also held by Locke) that Indians did not cultivate the land and thus had no right of ownership.[4] But amending Locke's view of what counts as mixing labour with land may not be worth the effort. His theory faces more serious difficulties.[5]

Right of ownership is in fact a bundle of rights, which includes the right to use a piece of property, dispose of its resources, exclude others, sell it or give it to others. A theory of acquisition which justifies some of these rights may not justify others. We might agree that 'mixing their labour with the land' can give individuals or groups the right to use at least some of its resources for their own purposes. But it does not follow that they have the right to use these resources in any way they please, to exclude everyone else from using them, or to transfer them to whomever they choose. Why shouldn't possessions revert to the common stock once a person has died or is no longer using them? Why should individuals or members of a group be able to claim land just because it was unjustly taken from their ancestors?[6] Historical title, even if it exists, might not be the sort of thing that can persist once people are separated from their acquisitions. But even if historical titles to possessions do persist over time, it does not follow that reparation for unjust dispossession requires that stolen property be returned to its original owner. It is noteworthy that Robert Nozick, though a supporter of reparation for historical injustice, would not think it unjust to give the Sioux money in place of their ancestral lands.

Let us suppose that a theory like Locke's manages to justify the full range of property rights. This justification would allow us to say that individuals or nations acquire a title to land by being the first to occupy and use a territory, or by inheriting it from those who first acquired it, or by it obtaining it by (uncoerced) gift or treaty from the original possessors or their heirs.[7] Any attempt to put the account to work in the service of reparative claims of nations faces an obvious practical difficulty. Nations and individuals who now exist are not, for the most part, the original occupiers of their territory or their heirs, but have displaced others, often by conquest. The Sioux wrested the Black Hills from the Kiowa and the Crow not long before white settlers came on the scene. The Maori may have displaced people who were the original inhabitants of New Zealand. In every area of the world, wave after wave of invaders have expropriated land and political control from existing occupants. As a result, virtually no nation can establish that it has a historical title to the territory it occupies. In fact, we know that most cannot make this claim. A theory of entitlement that requires an unblemished history of possession is doomed to irrelevancy. Nozick throws up his hands in the face of this difficulty, and suggests that for the time being we should forget about historical title and distribute resources according to the requirements of equity.[8] But this is not a solution that would please the Sioux.

Even if we can get around the practical and philosophical difficulties that face a theory like Locke's, moral problems remain. 'We were here first', says Waldron, has always been an unpleasant way of denying present aspirations or resisting current claims of need.[9] It is a morally dubious justification, because it allows people who were lucky enough to be in a position to make an original acquisition, or to be heirs of those who were, to enjoy opportunities that others lack. It offends against the idea that everyone in our society should have equal standing and equal chances.[10] Locke, aware of the disadvantages that can fall on those who have no opportunity to appropriate resources, attaches a proviso to his theory. Legitimate acquisition, he insists, depends on there being 'as good left for others as that already possessed'.[11] Whenever this condition is not satisfied, property entitlements lose their legitimacy, and have to be reviewed.

How we should interpret this proviso is extremely controversial. Nozick insists on adjustments to, or restrictions on, holdings only in those cases where present property rights threaten the lives of others.[12] David Lyons, who believes that 'justice requires the establishment and maintenance of background conditions for fair bargains and agreements and for fair social arrangements generally',[13] insists on a more radical interpretation. Suppose, he says, that a shipwreck casts on the shore of an island nation some destitute people who have no prospect of rescue. The islanders, he thinks, should not only sustain the lives of the newcomers, but also give them equal access to the resources of the island. Anything less would condemn the newcomers to an economically and socially subordinate position into the indefinite future. Property holdings of indigenous islanders have to be diminished and adjusted to satisfy this demand.

The vulnerability of titles to considerations of equity makes Lyons doubt that Indian titles could have survived intact even if dispossession had never occurred. Circumstances have changed considerably since the days when Europeans first arrived in the New World. World population is much greater, and the demand for resources has increased. It is true that the islanders in his story surrendered their resources voluntarily, whereas Indian land was taken by force. But Lyons does not think that the fact that Indians and other indigenous people were robbed of their land makes a significant difference to what justice now requires.

To persuade us that this is so, he asks us to imagine that the newcomers to the island were not peaceful refugees, but piratical invaders, who pushed aside the native people and seized most of their land and resources. This act of aggression was a crime. The pirates should have been punished, made to leave the island, and to pay for the damage they did, but, as is so often the case, there was no one capable of exacting these punishments. But this chapter of history is finished. The descendants of the pirates are not at all like their ancestors. They treat the native people as equal citizens, and property is now equitably distributed between individuals in the two groups. Lyons thinks that the happy ending to his story leaves the descendants of victims with no basis for reparation claims. 'If the generation in question has been deprived of no part of its own fair share of the island's resources, if they suffer no continuing disadvantage owing to the legacy of the former system on the island, what relevant matter might have been overlooked?'[14]

In the case of American Indians and other indigenous peoples, history has not had such a happy ending. But Lyons nevertheless thinks that his story tells us what justice now requires. Indigenous people, because of historical wrongs, have been deprived of their fair share of resources. Justice demands that their disadvantages be removed, but they have no inherited entitlement to the resources that their ancestors once possessed. 'The original rights of Native Americans were no more sacrosanct than anyone else's. From the fact that they had morally defensible claims two hundred or four hundred years ago it cannot be inferred that those claims persist.'[15] This does not mean that Lyons is unsympathetic to Indian land claims. He thinks that return of some of their lands would be a good means of alleviating their poverty, and thus achieving justice as equity. What Lyons doesn't say, but what his view allows, is that requirements of equity might be satisfied perfectly well by giving Indian tribes land somewhere else or by supplying them with money and other resources.

Right of possession

A case for land rights based on historical title faces serious difficulties. However, philosophical discussions of title do not generally distinguish between rights of ownership that in our society are possessed by individuals, corporations and other associations over particular pieces of land, buildings, personal items, capital, etc. and the right of a nation to exercise sovereignty over a territory: to make and enforce the law of its land, including laws about property. I will call the first 'right of ownership', and the second 'right of possession'. Since the Sioux constitute a nation, and their ancestral territory is the land once governed by their people, it seems better to understand their claim as asserting a right of possession over the Black Hills, rather than merely a title to property. The question is whether this makes their demand any easier to defend.

Possession, suggests Michael Walzer, is justified not (simply) by labour, but by the importance to members of a nation of their national life ('it had to be made somewhere').[16] Their ability to govern themselves according to their laws, maintain their institutions, and defend their rights depend on their being able to make the law of the land they are in: that is, to possess it. He admits that right of possession, like right of property, has moral limitations. The possession by a nation of vast reaches of land is problematic 'unless it can be tied in some plausible way to the requirements of national survival and political independence'.[17] But right of possession is less likely than right of ownership to be affected by demands of equity. Members of a nation can in most cases find a way to satisfy the Lockean proviso without surrendering their territory. They can take in refugees or allow other people to settle and acquire property in their territory (as in Lyons's story of the castaways). They can share their wealth with poor nations.

A nation's right of possession is generally compatible with allowing members of another nation to own property within its borders. An indigenous nation could assert right of possession over a territory without requiring all present landholders to leave or to give up all their existing economic activities. This difference between right of possession and right of property alleviates, even if it doesn't solve, one of the problems associated with historical title. But it does not get us much closer to justifying the Sioux claim. People of a nation have to live their common life somewhere, and this means, Walzer thinks, that they have a right to live it where they are. But it does not follow that they have a right to repossess territory taken from their ancestors.

However, there is a further difference between ownership and possession which does seem to provide a case for repossession. The common life that people of a nation value does not merely belong to existing members. A nation is an intergenerational association, and its laws, institutions and the territory over which the laws extend are supposed to be the inheritance of future generations. Unlike property, which can in most cases be sold, bequeathed or given away according to the desire of the owner, we generally suppose that the territory possessed by a nation cannot be disposed of as leaders or citizens please. This is because we assume that the people of a nation have an obligation to pass on their collective resources, their institutions and sources of wealth, to future members. This obligation might be overridden by other considerations. The people of a poor nation might decide that their descendants would be better off if they gave up their territory and moved elsewhere. Moreover, we know of lots of historical cases where nations have sold part of their territory to others or ceded it by treaty. But these exchanges (except where the transactions have been less than voluntary) usually presuppose the retention of 'the land where people walk' – or, as Walzer has it, the territory in which they have their homes.

If it were merely resources that present generations have been wrongfully deprived of by the dispossession of their forebears, then monetary compensation and land to live on would surely be adequate reparation. But the national inheritance that is passed down through the generations does not consist merely of the means of life. It often includes resources that cannot be separated from the land in which they are located. People of a nation learn to structure their lives around the activities that their land makes possible. They alter it to suit their purposes: they construct dwellings and monuments; they bury their dead in its soil and establish institutions that take a physical form. They imbue the features of the land with meaning; it features in their myths and becomes central to their traditions and spiritual life. The development of their culture is influenced by geography; the landscape plays an essential role in their stories and legends. They read off their history from landmarks and find their symbols in natural features. In short, the inheritance that members of each generation are supposed to pass on to their successors is inseparably bound up with the possession of a particular territory.

Descendants of members of a nation learn the skills appropriate to making a living from their land; they are taught to revere customs associated with a particular place. Moreover, transgenerational projects and activities associated with national life, the ways in which people of a nation choose to use their collective resources over a period of time, often depend on continuing possession of a particular territory. So it could be argued that when a nation is dispossessed, this is not only a great evil to its existing members; it harms their successors, robbing them of the inheritance to which they are entitled, and by so doing disrupts their ability to carry on their common life. Nothing but the return of their national territory counts as appropriate reparation for this wrong.

How persuasive is this argument? It applies most convincingly to the more immediate descendants of the dispossessed – those who have been brought up with the expectation that they will live in a particular land. And it accords with our intuitions about some cases. Tibet was occupied by the Chinese fifty years ago, and most Tibetans living now had not yet been born when the invasion occurred. Yet those who think that China acted unjustly also think that the Tibetans, many of whom are living in exile, have a continuing moral right of possession. Similarly, many people believe that the Palestinians ought to be able to return to the land which they or their parents were forced to abandon – even though many Palestinians have never lived in this land or even seen it.

However, a historical title that depends on the persistence of a lack that can only be filled by repossession of a territory has obvious limitations. Less immediate successors who grew up in a new place and had the opportunity to adjust their expectations to the opportunities of their new environment have less justification for claiming the territory of their ancestors, if any at all. The common life of a nation, like the lives of individuals, is adaptable. With this in mind, we can imagine a happier ending to the story of the Sioux. Let us suppose that at the beginning of the twentieth century the American government, recognizing the injustice of its relation to indigenous people, had embarked on a programme designed to overcome the disadvantages of the Sioux and other Indian nations. Members of the nation were given a large and fertile area of land and resources to build up their political and economic institutions. While retaining their religious beliefs, some of their laws and customs, and a considerable amount of political independence, the Sioux then became prosperous ranchers. (The Sioux have shown no interest in agriculture, but are said to have an inclination toward cattle raising.) Their new territory, the basis of their prosperity and their hopes for their children, has become their national homeland, and it figures more and more in their ceremonies and the stories they tell about themselves.

What more can reparation require? But if we admit that the Sioux in this alternative history have no title to the Black Hills, then (using the same reasoning as Lyons) how can we suppose that they have it as things are?

Ancestral land and sacred sites

One way of resisting the conclusion reached in the last section is to point to connections between a land and a people that do seem to persist through many generations.

> Many of the aboriginal claims in New Zealand, Australia, and North America, have to do with burial grounds or lands which have some other symbolic or religious significance. Religions and cultural trad-itions we know are very resilient, and the claim that the lost lands form the center of a present way of life – and remain sacred objects despite their loss – may be as credible a hundred years on as it was at the time of the dispossession.[18]

'Paha Sapa, the Black Hills, was the centre of the world, the place of God and holy mountains, where warriors went to speak with the Great Spirit and await visions.'[19] In Australian Aboriginal societies the origin of the people from the land, expressed in their law and religion, gives members immutable responsibilities and entitlements in respect to particular pieces of land. This connection with the land is so defining of an Aboriginal nation that it is not likely to disappear so long as the nation survives in any form.

Though members of indigenous nations are obvious examples of people who claim to have an enduring spiritual connection to a place, they are not the only ones who do so. Churches important to the Serbian religious heritage exist in Kosovo. Jerusalem contains churches, temples, mosques and other shrines that are of great importance to Jews, Christians and Moslems.

Let us allow that persisting religious and perhaps other strong cultural connections to a particular place can give rise to an entitlement. But what kind of entitlement is it? It seems unlikely that it is a title to possess the territory where these sacred sites exist. Nothing about the religious significance of the monuments or sites seems to require this. A more plausible idea is that people of a nation should have access to their religious sites, the right to protect them from harm and, perhaps, responsibility for their upkeep. In particular, they should be able to veto developments that would destroy them or undermine their religious significance. In fact, the land rights claimed by many indigenous communities are these limited rights to have access to, and control over, sacred sites and burial grounds. If these rights are generally recognized in world society, then they will limit what people of a nation can do to sites in their territory that are sacred to another nation. But they will not give a nation the right to repossess a territory.

Suppose that a whole land is sacred to a dispossessed nation. Indigenous people do not, after all, make a sharp distinction between economic and religious activities or between the law and religion. So it might be argued that the only way in which such a nation can regain its religious values and protect them from harm is for it to occupy and make the law for its ancestral territory. The Sioux may be among those who can plausibly make this claim. I would not want to rule out this possibility. However, if the Sioux had been compensated for dispossession, as in the story above, and if in addition they had been given access to sacred sites in the Black Hills and the ability to protect these sites from harm, would it still be plausible for them to claim that they were entitled to the Black Hills? Given the resilience of nations and the proved ability of people to adapt to new conditions, I have difficulty supposing that this entitlement would persist.

However, the difficulty may simply be a consequence of my limitations as a philosopher who has been trained in a particular tradition and is accustomed to European ways of thinking. James Tully argues that attempts to apply Western philosophical theories, including theories about historical title, to the land claims of indigenous people not only misrepresent them, but also fail to respect the laws and customs that are the basis for these claims.[20] An obligation to respect the land rights of the people of a nation, he thinks, is entailed by a respect for their right to live according to their own law. Since the Sioux and the people of other indigenous nations claim their ancestral land as their entitlement according to their law, it seems to follow from Tully's position that a settlement compatible with respect would honour this entitlement.

Tully is not claiming that all titles based on law and custom should be accepted uncritically. Law, including the laws of indigenous people, can have unjust consequences. The indigenous people of Fiji maintain communal control over most of the land in their country according to a law that operates to the detriment of the descendants of people from India who were settled on the island by the British during the nineteenth century. Indian Fijians are in a vulnerable economic and political position, because of a handicap created and maintained by law.[21] Tully is not committed to supporting native Fijians just because their law gives them the right to most of the land. His position can be interpreted as reconciliatory, as aiming for an outcome that nations can accept as a basis for their relationship in a federal system that assumes equality of nations.

But the equality of nations, which is the moral starting point for his reflections, does not tell us what settlement counts as fair in those cases where people of nations make contrary claims. Whose law should prevail in the land once occupied by the Sioux? If the Sioux were offered more adequate recompense for their loss, would it be reasonable for them to continue to claim their ancestral land? The requirement of equal respect will not by itself provide an answer. What we want, as suggested before, is a settlement that all sides, from their respective points of view, can regard as just (an overlapping consensus). This requires that all participants appeal to, and critically examine, their ideas about what is rational and right, as well as make an attempt to understand the viewpoint of the others. There is nothing wrong with making use of the concepts and theories of Western philosophy to argue about the validity of land claims, if only to determine whether those who belong to this tradition can find grounds for accepting them.

Memory and history

The arguments of the last two sections provide limited support for those who claim land unjustly taken from their ancestors. They support the right to repossession of immediate descendants of the dispossessed and the entitlement of people of a nation to have access to, and rights with respect to, landmarks of spiritual importance that exist in the territory of another nation. The problem with these entitlements is not merely that they are too limited to underwrite claims like those made by the Sioux. The reasons I have offered in support of them depart significantly from what is needed to justify a historical title of the kind defended by Locke, with a consequent weakening of the case for reparation for historical injustices.

The entitlements in question are based on the needs of the successors of the dispossessed – not on a historical act of acquisition by forebears that gives their successors rights in perpetuity. People who have been brought up to live in a particular land, and whose spiritual and cultural ties to it remain strong, have a need which only repossession can satisfy. People with a strong spiritual connection to particular landmarks or sites have a need to retain that connection. The entitlements I have defended answer to these needs. Recognizing them amounts to an acknowledgement by the people of a political society, or the world as a whole, that these needs are important and ought to be satisfied, all things being equal. Such needs, however, can disappear in the course of time, or they may be satisfied in different ways. They are not something that can give people an inextinguishable right to a property or possession. Moreover, it is not obvious that satisfying them has to be regarded as reparation for a past wrong. Descendants of pirates and victims on Lyons's island should take into account such needs when they are distributing resources according to requirements of equity. To be equitable, a society has to allow for the fact that individuals need different things. But there seems no reason why descendants of the pirates should suppose that in respecting these needs, and the entitlements to which they give rise, they are making reparation for past injustices.

Suppose that a long drought forces the inhabitants to abandon their island and seek refuge somewhere else. They leave voluntarily, though reluctantly; no one has done them an injustice. The drought lasts for fifty years, and throughout that time the people of the island, though comfortably settled in another land, have never lost hope of return and have brought up their children accordingly. When the island recovers, we would probably assume (even without the assurance provided by a Lockean deed of title) that the islanders, though they consist largely of people who have never seen their ancestral homeland, should be able to return. If the climate of the island has changed permanently, and the island has subsequently been inhabited by a group of people more able to cope with arid conditions, we would probably want to insist that the original islanders should have access to the sacred landmarks that they were forced to leave behind.

A need is a need, however caused. Why, then, should we regard the cases of the Sioux and the Tibetan exiles as different from the situation of the islanders? The obvious answer is that the victims of injustice and their successors regard these cases as different. Members of nations whose forebears suffered wrong remember how their injuries occurred; they resent injustices done to their nation and regard themselves as being injured not just by being deprived of the land they love, but also by the lack of respect for their nation shown by the perpetrators. Memory of historical injustice is not a trivial matter that can be ignored by those concerned with undoing present inequities. Remembrance, says Waldron, is important to the identity of individuals and communities.

> To neglect the historical record is to do violence to this identity and thus to the community that it sustains. And since communities help generate a deeper sense of identity for the individuals they comprise, neglecting or expunging the historical record is a way of undermining and insulting individuals as well.[22]

Moreover, an injury to an identity can cause or compound other harms. Members of nations whose ancestors were the victims of unrequited historical wrongs often suffer from despair, depression and loss of both confidence and hope for the future. Even the material disadvantages that result from historical injustice are viewed by the people who suffer them from the perspective of their history. The Sioux, for example, make a connection between their present state of deprivation and the suffering of their ancestors, who preferred to starve rather than give up their land.

Harms that are intrinsically historical – which cannot be separated from the way people view their history – call for a reparative response that addresses this history. They require that the perpetrators or their successors acknowledge these wrongs, and that they bring it about that the harm caused by the injustice no longer stands in the way of respectful and trusting relations. Given that the harms suffered by the Sioux cannot be separated in their account of their history from unjust dispossession, the most appropriate reparation is surely to return to them some of their ancestral lands, along with the resources they need to maintain their communal life. What cannot be justified by an appeal to historical title, or by concentrating merely on needs, can be justified by recognizing the importance to people of their history and by taking a reconciliatory approach to reparative justice.

This conclusion is supported by some notable differences between the imagined history of the Sioux and their actual history. In the imagined history, earlier acts of reparation have brought it about that respectful and just relations exist between the successors of the perpetrators and the descendants of the victims. It should be noted that a conviction that justice has been done is compatible with a belief that the recompense made to the Sioux at the beginning of the twentieth century (according to the story) was not adequate. Yet, it improved the well-being of the Sioux, and gave them the motivation to make adaptive changes to their economic and cultural life. It also gradually improved relations with non-indigenous Americans. From the perspective of the present, reconciliation in this case has been a historical process, each generation building on the progress achieved by its predecessors.

In the actual history of the Sioux, the situation is very different. The injustice of dispossession was compounded by other injustices and, in more recent times, by neglect and a refusal of the US government to face up to past injustices. Reparation was unsatisfactory and was provided only because of a court ruling. Under the circumstances the injustices of the past continue to rankle. As a result, the Sioux have come to see their history as a series of injustices that resulted from their wrongful dispossession from the Black Hills. This dispossession made them especially vulnerable to the government policies which had such a detrimental effect on their standard of living and communal life. It forced them to fight a long battle to have their claim taken seriously. Their national identity, their ability to take pride in their history, and their hopes for a meaningful future for their children have thus come to focus on their fight for rectification of this initial injustice – for the return of their ancestral land. The harm to their identity caused by a history of injustice makes it appropriate for them to make this demand, and for the successors of the perpetrators to fulfil it.

There are two immediate objections to this line of reasoning. The first questions whether the harms require a reparative response. Why not regard harms to identity as creating needs that can be satisfied by a variety of means? Why not send in an army of psychologists or grief counsellors to administer to the Sioux and others harmed by their history? Why can't people with injured identities be encouraged to forget the past and live for the future, or at least to concentrate on the more positive aspects of their history? The second is a doubt about how seriously we should take the claims of people who have nurtured for generations a sense of being wronged. People of a nation can identify with a history that is more mythological than real. They can become obsessive about some aspects of their past. Are we required to return ancestral land just because the people of a nation have become fixated on getting it back?

The first objection assumes that having an identity affected by remembrance is simply a psychological state of affairs subject to manipulation. With suitable therapy it can be made to disappear or change its nature; a demagogue or a psychologist might work on it for his own purposes. However, the form of identity relevant to justice as reparation has a moral dimension, and is subject to moral assessment. A sense of identity shaped by their nation's history is not simply something that many individuals happen to have – something that might become less of a hindrance to good relations or even dispensed with altogether if only people could be persuaded to think more positively about their present and future. A sense of history is something that members of a nation are morally required to cultivate. The reason has nothing to do with the kind of patriotism or nationalism which requires that members identify with their nation and its past, but with considerations discussed in the first two chapters. To be worthy of respect, a nation has to be prepared to fulfil its historical responsibilities. This means that its members have to be prepared to keep its commitments and make reparations for its past wrongs – including wrongs that were done in past generations. Fulfilling this requirement depends on members regarding the past of their nation as a source of obligation and entitlement. Some members may be more prepared to fulfil this requirement than others. But the point is that they ought to fulfil it, and that doing so requires having a memory that is sensitive to the historical obligations of their nation. If members of nations are expected to remember their historical obligations and regard them as morally important, then it would be absurd – for logical as well as psychological reasons – to insist that they should forget about their historical entitlements or regard them as being of little importance. The rule that 'like cases ought to be treated alike' applies in both directions. I cannot suppose that an injustice done to another is less of a wrong than the same injustice done to me; nor can I suppose that an injustice done to me is less of a wrong than the same injustice done to another.

Remembrance of events that have to do with the obligations and entitlements of a nation is thus part of what could be described as the 'moral identity' of its members. The importance of having such an identity explains why their remembrance ought to be treated with respect, and not as an unfortunate psychological condition subject to treatment or manipulation. It makes intelligible the indignation, anger or shame with which members of nations commonly respond to injustices in their history, and why we think that it is proper for them to respond in these ways. It explains why demoralization and other harms to the common life of a nation are the likely result of a history of injustices, especially when the wrongdoers refuse to acknowledge that wrong was done. Not to be treated with proper respect is a harm to moral identity.

The second objection – that a view of reparation which relies on the historical perspective of members of nations will be held hostage to those with historical grudges – is partially answered by the above discussion. A theory of reparation as reconciliation assigns duties to both parties, and does not countenance intransigence or the making of unreasonable demands. It insists that demands be just, and in this chapter some progress has been made in determining what form of reparation counts as just and when demands for reparation are not justified.

We don't have to think that every nation that has been dispossessed of territory sometime in its history is entitled to have it returned. In the imaginary history, nothing more is owed to the Sioux once the harm to their nation and the damage to relationships caused by the injustice have been overcome. Members of their community have gained the resources they need to maintain their common life, and their obtaining these things is the result of acts of reparation by the successors of the wrongdoers. If some members of the nation continue to insist that the Black Hills belongs to them, justice does not support their claim. They have no historical title, and the harm to their nation – including the harm caused to their moral identity by acts of disrespect – has been appropriately addressed by past acts of reparation. The reconciliatory approach eliminates from the scope of reparation historical wrongs that have either lost their significance or been superseded by more positive historical developments. The reconciliatory approach allows that injustices can be buried by history.

However, injustices that took place a long time ago are not always buried. Some injustices have rankled for centuries; enmities have lasted for generations. Furthermore, members of nations can have very different, and contrary, views about whether injustices have been superseded by more recent developments. Their views about the nature of the injustices, and whether reparative justice has been achieved, can also be at odds. In the next chapter I will consider how difficulties associated with the passage of time and differences of perspective should be met.

5

A Matter of Time

In the Middle Ages the Serbian kingdom under the Nemanja dynasty extended over what is now Serbia, Albania, eastern Bosnia and Macedonia. It was a major centre of Orthodox Christianity. A coalition led by Serbian Prince Lazar was defeated by a much larger Turkish force in the Battle of Kosovo in 1389. The subsequent Turkish invasion brought the kingdom to an end several decades later. The Battle of Kosovo took place more than 600 years ago, but for Serbs whose claim to Kosovo is justified by reference to the territory ruled by the Nemanjas, 'it is as if it occurred yesterday'.[1]

Common sense tells us that time should make a difference to the validity or reasonableness of historical claims. Six hundred years, most of us think, is enough to put a claim to territory or compensation for loss of territory out of contention, even if there is no other reason for rejecting it. Common sense also endorses an order of considerability among past injustices. More recent injustices are assumed to take precedence over more ancient wrongs. Prime Minister Blair thought that he should apologize for British behaviour during the Irish potato famine, but didn't feel called upon to express regret for the assaults on the Irish by Cromwell, let alone Elizabeth I. Presumably, he thought that the passage of time had rendered these earlier injustices less salient, less demanding of an act of contrition. But not everyone agrees with these intuitions. To Serbian nationalists the fact that the Nemanjan kingdom existed so long ago is irrelevant. For some Irish the punitive invasion by Cromwell still rankles.

Those who insist on complaining about ancient wrongs cannot be dismissed as irrational – at least, not without further justification. For

I have argued that the way people remember their history is relevant to the validity of their reparative claims, and wrongs that took place *centuries* ago can play a central role in the historical narratives of nations – as in the case of the Serbs. Many claims that refer to ancient wrongs have been invalidated by more recent historical events, but it does not follow that none of them is justified. We cannot simply assume that the passage of time puts an end to reparative entitlements and responsibilities.

In any case, common sense does not speak with one voice. We are prepared to believe that some of our historical obligations persist indefinitely. Treaty obligations, unless a time limit is built into them, are assumed to be perpetual. 'Some existing British treaties have endured for nearly six centuries, and many for three.'[2] That such obligations tend to persist is underwritten by the arguments I used to support their existence. Since the keeping of agreements is a trans-generational responsibility, which gives members of one generation an obligation to keep the commitments of their predecessors, there is no apparent temporal limit to how far down through the generations the responsibility extends – no reason why an obligation should not be transmitted indefinitely. Changes to conditions or to the interests of the parties can eventually make agreements obsolete, but this does not necessarily happen in all cases, or may not happen for a very long time. But if obligations to keep agreements are perpetual (all things being equal), then how can we avoid the conclusion that obligations to make reparation for violations of agreements and similar wrongs also perpetuate themselves through the generations until they are finally discharged? Present circumstances may make it impossible or unnecessary to fulfil this responsibility, but we cannot suppose that this will be so in all cases. So the task is not simply to defend common sense from those who make demands for reparation for ancient wrongs. We also have to square this common sense with an equally commonsensical view that our historical obligations to keep commitments are not subject to a statute of temporal limitation. I will explain in this chapter how the difficulties may be resolved.

Existence and responsibility

Commitments of nations are perpetual. There is no temporal limitation to their scope. Nevertheless, they do not last for ever. Conditions change. Nations come and go; they undergo radical political changes; they are conquered or incorporated into larger units. I have pointed out that an obligations-dependent approach provides a simple way of discounting some reparative claims. The historical obligations and entitlements that I have been concerned with in this part of the study belong to nations as responsible political agents. So it seems reasonable to dismiss some reparative claims, including those made by the Serbs, by pointing out that once a nation has ceased to exist, or has been radically transformed, then its obligations and entitlements also cease to exist. No one has an obligation to keep the treaties that it made. No reparative claims can be made against it or on its behalf. Continued existence is a necessary condition for having a historical entitlement or obligation. It seems no more likely that the citizens of modern Turkey (or anyone else) are responsible for making reparation for injustices committed by the Ottomans six centuries ago than that the citizens of modern Greece are responsible for the deeds of the ancient Athenians. And the connection between the Nemanja kingdom and modern Serbia is probably too tenuous to support any reparative entitlement.

This reasoning depends on the premiss that a 'nation', in the relevant sense, is a political agent capable of making and keeping agreements. One of the implications of this assumption is that a group of people cannot declare themselves to be the rightful possessors of the territory of a nation that no longer exists just because they have an ancestral, linguistic or cultural connection with its members. It is true that the term 'nation' is often used in a way that suggests that such a claim can be made. A nation is sometimes said to be a group defined by a culture, language or religion, and these things often survive in some form even when the nation as a political agent has disappeared. But this way of using the term is not relevant to a theory of historical obligations and entitlements. A cultural group cannot pursue policies or make and keep promises. It cannot assume the responsibilities of a political agent, and thus it cannot have the obligations or entitlements associated with agenthood. The arguments I have used in this part of my investigation to support reparative claims for historical injustices cannot be used by non-political associations or by nations that have no political connection to the nation wronged. If the people in these associations have been disadvantaged by their history, this may give them a good case for compensation on grounds of equity. But that is another matter.[3]

Many claims based on ancient injustices can be dismissed using the obligations-dependent view of reparation that I defended in chapter 3. But this strategy, though intuitively appealing, brings us face to face with an obvious difficulty. If having a political or organizational connection with the nation (or organized group of another kind) that made an agreement or suffered or inflicted a wrong is a necessary condition for having a historical entitlement or obligation, how do we determine when this condition is fulfilled? The answer is not always obvious. The British government made and broke the Treaty of Waitangi before the state of New Zealand came into existence. So it is reasonable to wonder how non-Maori New Zealanders can be held responsible for making reparation for a wrong done by the British. The fact that Queen Elizabeth II made an official apology for injustices against the Maori suggests that responsibility falls on the British. Even if New Zealand, for whom Elizabeth is also Queen, is a historical extension of British rule, the United States is certainly not.[4] One of the complaints of American colonists against their British rulers was that British recognition of the Indian nations (as embodied in the Royal Commission Report) prevented settlers from moving into the Ohio Valley and other regions deemed to belong to Indian tribes. Was the American nation, once it broke with its colonial past, no longer morally required to adhere to the agreements made by the British with the Indians?

Even more serious questions arise concerning the identity of indigenous nations. In Australia, governments, settlers and missionaries undermined or severely compromised the ability of indigenous people to govern themselves according to their own law and to maintain their national integrity. Some Aboriginal nations have survived more or less intact, though they are far from being independent political entities. Other Aboriginal communities are the remnants of nations, or are made up of people from different nations. There is a political body with limited powers elected by Aborigines to represent them in Australian federal politics. The question raised by this situation is whether any of these groups has a sufficient political connection to the nations that were dispossessed to be in the position to make legitimate reparative claims.

Questions about the persistence of national identity awaken more radical doubts. The problem of establishing political identity is most obvious in cases where there was an abrupt and radical break in political continuity. Revolutionary political changes or invasions create obvious problems for a theory of historical entitlement and obligation. But evolutionary change can be just as problematic. Over time members of nations alter their policies, alliances, institutions and other features of what Walzer describes as 'common life'. Britain of 600 years ago was different in important respects from the Britain of today. So why should we think that the Britain of today retains responsibilities incurred 600 years ago? Why should we ever think that the nation that made a treaty is continuous with the one that broke it? Or that the nation that suffered or committed a wrong is the same as the one now making or facing demands for reparation?

The transgenerational continuum

Holding an individual responsible for past actions hinges on the belief that she is identical with the person who did those deeds, and so philosophers have tried to provide reasons for assuming that a presently existing person really is the same as her younger self. It is natural to think that the above questions about the responsibilities of nations must be answered by reference to criteria of national identity over time. Philosophical precedents suggest that providing such criteria would be a difficult undertaking, with little hope of a decisive, uncontroversial result. Fortunately, we can avoid most of the difficulties. Our concern is not whether a nation at one time is the same or different from a nation at another time, but whether the obligations or entitlements possessed by people of the past have become the obligations and entitlements of their successors. The crux of the matter is not the identity of the agent, but continuity of responsibility for particular agreements or acts. Obligations and entitlements can be passed from the members of one nation to members of the nation that succeeds it. Australia, Canada and New Zealand formally or tacitly took over many of the responsibilities that British administrations had incurred. That is why it is reasonable to assume that New Zealand inherited responsibility for the Treaty of Waitangi. Even in cases where political separation has been more like an acrimonious divorce or where revolutionary upheavals have changed the interests and policies of a nation, we cannot assume that the continuity on which responsibility depends has ceased to exist. The issue is not whether a nation has become something different as the result of political change, but whether, and in what respect, the interests, relationships and moral requirements on which a particular obligation or entitlement is predicated continue to exist.

In making judgements about whether a particular responsibility survives political change, it is reasonable to begin with the presumption of survival. The burden of proof should fall on those who deny continuity of responsibility. People of other nations are entitled to trust that our agreements will be kept, that relations of respect and the understandings that arise from them will persist, that their interests and entitlements will be respected, and that they will receive reparation for injustice. Changes that occur with time may affect the way obligations and entitlements are interpreted; they may render some agreements obsolete. But we should presume that relations of respect that ought to lie behind these particular agreements and understandings, and the obligations that arise from maintaining these relations, persist.

Nevertheless, the continuity that depends on each generation passing on responsibilities to the next can be disrupted. Two criteria can be used to determine whether this has happened in a particular case. The first focuses on legal and institutional changes. The continuity is likely to be broken with respect to particular relationships and responsibilities when, as a result of political changes, the laws, institutions or practices that have in the past governed these relationships and responsibilities cease to exist or are radically altered. Secession or revolution will generally bring about such an alteration, but it is important to recognize that continuity can be disrupted in some spheres of political activity while surviving in others. When the United States freed itself from British rule, its citizens lost any responsibility they might have had for making good on agreements that Britain had made with nations such as France or Spain. Continuity in foreign affairs was upset by the political events which produced the independent nation. Americans had to develop their own practice of dealing with foreign nations according to their interests and situation. But the American Revolution left largely untouched relationships and interests on its internal frontier. Not only did the legal system remain largely the same; Indians and settlers retained the same interests and concerns. In most localities relations did not alter very much at all: the same people continued to interact with each other in the same ways. The same officials carried out their responsibilities. The moral reasons for mutual respect and co-operation remained the same. Under the circumstances, it was reasonable, from a moral point of view, for the parties to assume that existing agreements remained valid and that previously incurred obligations still existed.

The second criterion focuses on the relation between the government of a political society and the governed. Commitment making, I have argued, presupposes that nations are able to regard each other with respect. If a nation fails to satisfy one of the conditions for being worthy of respect, then the agreements it makes will be either invalid, untrustworthy or seriously deficient. Agreements made with governments that do not represent the interests of their people are obviously deficient. Members of a nation should not be expected to keep the agreements or make reparations for the crimes committed by a ruler who acted against their interests and over which they or their predecessors had no control. If a revolution overthrows such a ruler, then the revolutionary government should not be held responsible for what he has done. However, dictators can rule with the consent of the governed or represent their interests, and sometimes the people of the nation are accessories to their crimes, or this may be true of some deeds, but not others. When the people have shown their support for, or participated in, making agreements or committing crimes, they cannot so easily divest themselves of responsibility when the regime changes.

A criterion which absolves people from responsibility for some of the actions of dictators is intuitively plausible, but often difficult to apply. The Germans voted Hitler into office; many of them supported his dictatorship, at least for a period of time. Some participated actively in the crimes of the regime, or acted in ways that made it possible for them to be committed. For these reasons most people judge that German citizens have rightly been required to accept responsibility for making reparations to victims of the Nazis. According to this view, breaking with the Nazi past and setting up a new state did not absolve the German people of responsibility for the past. After the Russian Revolution in 1917, the Soviet government decided not to be bound by treaties made by the Tsarist government with Britain and France, and made a separate peace with Germany. This action seems easier to justify. The people of Tsarist Russia never had a chance to control or choose those who made important decisions of state. Though they went along with the these decisions – by allowing themselves to be mobilized for war – there was so little opportunity for most people to become politically informed, let alone active, that their acceptance of Tsarist edicts probably cannot count as consent. The Soviet government, at least at this stage, probably did represent the will of most of the people.

Both these conclusions could be disputed for philosophical as well as historical reasons. It is not easy to make a judgement about whether a government has the consent of the governed in societies where people have never been allowed a choice or where dissent is likely to be punished. In any case, the criteria of respectability that I presented in chapter 2 do not tell us exactly what counts as 'consent of the governed'. Nevertheless, the presumption of continuity means that members of a nation cannot shrug off responsibilities incurred by their leaders simply by changing their political orientation and declaring that they are starting afresh.

The presumption that obligations and entitlements persist is also likely to give indigenous communities the benefit of the doubt when their status as continuing nations is questioned. As a result of European incursions, indigenous nations ceased to be the independent nations described by the British Royal Commission, and retained at best a limited authority to govern themselves. In many cases, as described above, indigenous communities have ceased to be nations in any real sense, or they have formed new political structures. Some communities have been so traumatized by a history of exploitation and suppression that they lack the ability or resources to enforce their law or protect their common life. Should we assume that indigenous people, at least in cases where political discontinuity has been radical, have lost the historical entitlements that were once possessed by their nation?

There are both pragmatic and moral reasons for rejecting this assumption. Nations, unlike individuals, can be resurrected, and for governments concerned about the well-being of indigenous populations, allowing or encouraging resurrection may be the best political and moral option. This is the lesson that might be drawn from the failure of policies of integration so vigorously pursued by Australia, Canada and the United States during the early part of the last century. But there is another moral reason for resurrecting nations and presuming that their members inherit the entitlements of their forebears. Non-indigenous members of states were responsible for the degradation of indigenous nations, and appropriate reparation in many cases would be to allow and encourage resurrection of nations, so long as indigenous people have distinct communities, want to live according to their law, and have resources over which they can exercise control. The fact that indigenous people may construct or make use of new political organizations does not get in the way of them being able to make reparative demands on behalf of the nations that previously existed. A new political society can be the legitimate heir of the entitlements and obligations of its predecessor.

Past injustices and present harms

The presumption, defended in the last section, that historical obligations and entitlements persist unless there are good reasons to deny their existence, is in conflict with the common-sense assumption that reparative entitlements and obligations fade away as time passes. We reasonably assume that those who deny that an agreement persists must accept the burden of proof. But in the case of reparation for historical injustices, common sense is inclined to insist that the burden of proving that an obligation persists belongs to those who make reparative claims. We are predisposed to believe that reparative entitlements lapse in the course of time. So our problem is not only to determine whether this common-sense assumption can be justified, but also to explain why we want to treat some claims based on history differently from others.

Common sense can sometimes be given a familiar legal defence. Since the accused in law is assumed to be innocent until proved guilty, the burden of proof will fall on the accuser. And since evidence tends to disappear, and memory becomes less reliable as an injustice recedes into the past, it is natural to suppose that the task of the accuser will become more difficult as time goes by. Legal systems often impose a statute of limitations on the cases they will consider. But the requirements of reparative justice are not the same as the requirements that apply to procedures for determining guilt or innocence (at least in criminal cases). If there is some doubt about who is responsible for a wrongdoing, then it is reasonable to demand that the accusers supply proof. However, in many cases where reparative claims are made, there is no doubt about the nature of the wrong or the identity of the guilty party. This is usually not the matter in dispute. When this is so, there seems to be no reason on grounds of availability of evidence to suppose that the passage of time makes any difference to the legitimacy of a claim.

There is, however, another way of defending common sense. Both restorative and reconciliatory approaches to reparation demand that harm done by an injustice to victims or their descendants be addressed and, if possible, removed. Justifying reparative claims depends on being able to make a connection between a past injustice and present harms. But if perpetual historical titles to property or possessions do not exist, then these harms will consist of the present suffering and disadvantages caused by the injustice. As time passes, the connection between present harms and historical injustices is likely to become more and more tenuous. As an injustice recedes into the distant past, it will become increasingly implausible to blame it for any conditions that exist in the present.

This intuitively attractive suggestion is developed by George Sher. Suppose, he says, that X, though a promising student, has been discriminatorily prevented from getting a place in law school. Though X knows that he will be able to gain entry in another year, he is discouraged by the rejection, and does not reapply. He finds a job and makes no further attempt to get educational qualifications. In a world where he had not been subject to unjust discrimination, X might have fared very differently. Let us assume that in this alternative world, X completes his law degree, gets a high-paying job in a law firm, and enjoys a successful career as a lawyer. Does this mean that X should receive in reparation the salary he would have earned if the injustice had not been done? Sher plausibly argues that X is not entitled to make such a claim. For how X fares in the alternative world depends on things that he does there: completing his degree and working hard in his profession. His entitlement to a high salary and status, in other words, arises from his actions in the alternative world, and not from anything that he did or was done to him in the actual world. His position in the actual world depends in part on his own actions: for example, his failure to reapply to law school. This does not mean that X is not entitled to any reparation. Because he was treated in a discriminatory way, he deserves recompense for loss of opportunity. But he is not entitled, says Sher, to what he would have gained if the injustice had not been done.[5]

Sher's point is that reparation is warranted only for what he calls the 'automatic effects' of the initial wrong act.[6] A similar limitation can be put on reparative obligations. Suppose that a factory worker is killed as the result of the negligence of his employer. The grief of members of the family and their loss of income are automatic effects of the injustice, and it is reasonable to suppose that the employer has an obligation to compensate the worker's family for their loss of his wages, and that he should do what he can to make their grief more easy to bear. Suppose, however, that the injustice causes further bad effects. The son of the family becomes so depressed as the consequence of his father's death that he drops out of university, joins a criminal gang, causes more grief to his family, and finally shoots someone while robbing a liquor store. Does the employer also have a responsibility for these harms? It is at least arguable that he bears responsibility for the son's depression and his failure at university. Attributions of responsibility are often contentious, and we usually decide such matters as best we can by going into the details of a particular case. But it does not seem plausible to blame the employer for the son joining a gang, causing grief to his family, or shooting someone in a robbery. These harms do not count as automatic effects of the injustice, and the employer has no reparative obligations with respect to them – even if we are sure that they would not have happened if the father had not been killed.

Sher does not tell us exactly what counts as an automatic effect. But since reparative responsibilities exist only if wrong has been done, automatic effects are probably best understood as those causal consequences of an injustice for which the perpetrator can be held responsible. The law school is responsible for X's loss of opportunity, but not for his failure to get a lawyer's salary. The employer is responsible for the family's financial loss and for their grief, but not for the son's criminal career. To specify when an agent through his action (or failure to act) is responsible for an effect is a difficult task – a contentious matter in both law and philosophy. But the difficulties do not prevent us from having a common-sense grasp of when responsibility exists and what is needed to attribute or question it.

Two conditions seem necessary and jointly sufficient. A causal effect for which a perpetrator can be held responsible is, first of all, an inevitable, natural or difficult-to-avoid result of his action or failure to act. Either the perpetrator intended that his act or failure to act would have this effect, or he should have known that it was probable. The financial loss of the worker's family is an inevitable effect of his death, but not his son's criminal behaviour. The second condition is that there is no other action, condition or failure to act to which the effect can more reasonably be attributed.[7] The son's decision to join a gang and X's failure to reapply to law school should (surely) be attributed at least in part to their own decisions, or to the failure of family members to act appropriately, or to inadequacies in the social environment. Sher's position, understood in these terms, is that perpetrators owe reparation to those suffering from the causal effects of an injustice only when (and only to the extent that) the harmful effects can be blamed on them. I will assume in the following discussion that he is right.

Using Sher's requirement we can, it seems, defend common-sense views about the effect of time on reparation claims. The amount of responsibility that can be attributed to an agent for the causal effects of an injustice tends to diminish with time as effects become attributable to other causes (including other injustices). If X had got a law degree and become a successful lawyer, his children's chances in life would be much better than they are. But the harm suffered by the children is less attributable to the original injustice than the harm suffered by X, and by the third generation there is likely to be no basis left for a reparative claim.

A consequence of Sher's position is that only the more immediate successors of those who were wronged have legitimate reparation claims (and in many cases there may be doubts even about *their* entitlements). This result, as he admits, has counter-intuitive implications. Injustices committed more than several generations ago – including many injustices to Indian nations – cannot be the subject of reparative claims.[8] Being driven out of the Black Hills, according to his reasoning, is not the injustice to which the present suffering of the Sioux should be attributed. The argument seems to be this. The harms caused by dispossession could have been alleviated by actions taken after the dispossession occurred. If, for example, the government had acted as I described in my imaginary history of the Sioux, these harms would probably not now exist. So presently existing harms should be regarded as the automatic effect of more recent policies of discrimination or neglect (or, some might say, of the refusal of the Sioux to use their compensation money to improve the standard of living of their community). If this reasoning is sound, then older injustices drop out of the picture, and only recent injustices remain as the subject of reparation claims.

History and meaning

Sher gives us a reason to discount ancient injustices, but at the cost of eliminating from consideration all wrongs but the more recent. People who support reparative claims such as those made by the Sioux will find this result difficult to accept. In fact, I do not think that Sher's attempt to put temporal limits on reparative entitlements is successful – at least to the extent he supposes. The reasons for rejecting it are implicit in the discussion of historical entitlements in the previous chapter. There are two closely related difficulties with the way in which he reaches his conclusion. He does not allow for the way in which injustices are connected in the history of a relationship between victims and perpetrators. And he operates with a limited and inadequate conception of harm.

Immediate causes are not necessarily the deeds we hold responsible for harms. According to the above definition of 'automatic effect', only independent actions (or failures to act) are causes to which harms can be attributed. The neighbour who brought the worker's family the news of his death was the immediate cause of the grief of the widow and her children. But their grief cannot be attributed to this act of communication. The tale-bearer was not responsible for their suffering (though he could have been guilty of insensitivity in the way he delivered the news). Conveying information is not an independent action. The nature of the news, the fact that it was told, has to be explained by reference to the injustice that it relates: in this case the death caused by the employer's negligence.

An act can be partially independent and yet intrinsically related to a prior injustice. Suppose that the factory owner refuses to compensate the worker's family, and that, as a result, its members continue to live in poverty. Refusal to make recompense is an additional injustice. It compounds the harm and causes further suffering. But it does not *replace* the earlier injustice as that to which the family's poverty should be attributed. Their suffering is still attributable to the wrongful death. More accurately, it should be attributed to a history of injustice that includes the original wrong and the refusal to compensate for it.

Ancient injustices to nations, as we have seen, often belong to an interconnected history of wrongs that ought to be treated as a whole for purposes of reparation. If a government refuses to acknowledge or make reparation for unjustly dispossessing an indigenous nation, these more recent injustices do not replace the original injustice as the wrongs to which present suffering should be attributed. They compound the wrong; they become part of a history of injustice and thereby relevant to demands for reparation. But their existence should not prevent members of the indigenous nation from demanding reparation for dispossession.

There are other ways, not mentioned in the previous chapter, in which injustices that happen over a period of time can be interdependent. They may be manifestations of an unjust policy pursued relentlessly by a nation over a long period of time. Or they may be the result of prejudice, an attitude of disrespect that persists through the generations and influences policies. The policies toward Aborigines adopted by Australian governments changed over time, but they had in common the assumption that Aborigines were racially and culturally inferior. In both types of cases, particular injustices are interdependent components of a history of disrespect – a history that cannot be understood without reference to its earlier as well as its later stages. It is this history, not just its most recent stages, that is relevant to reparative claims.[9]

The same conclusion follows from a closer look at the harms that can be attributed to historical injustices. A history that connects earlier and later injustices is not merely a chronicle of events. It is a narrative that makes sense of events at a particular time by reference to later or earlier happenings. What counts as harm, what kind of harm it is, depends on the way in which people understand their history. The Sioux experience their poverty in relation to their history. The material disadvantages or adverse psychological reactions that result from a history of injustices are not harms that could just as easily have resulted from another kind of cause. Their being the result of this history becomes intrinsic to the way in which they are experienced. But to the extent that this is so, then surely we must attribute the harm to this history – and thus to the events, distant as well as more recent, that play an essential role in the narrative.

This suggestion seems to confuse 'history' as a narrative with 'history' as a series of events. People are caused to suffer not merely by the events themselves, but by the ideas they get into their heads about these events. This way of putting the matter might be taken as a reason for attributing the sorrow and resentment felt by people of a wronged nation to their education. Opponents of reparative claims are in fact often ready to blame agitators or educators for using the past to inflame passions. Sometimes these accusations are justified. But attempts to deflect responsibility for harm on to more immediate causes will often fail. Automatic effects of injustice include responses that count as natural or proper – like the grief of the worker's family. The relationship between national identity and history (as noted in the previous chapter) makes it natural for members of a nation to feel sorrow or resentment about injustices done to their nation. This response is also morally appropriate in many cases. Members of nations, as I argued, are supposed to treat their history as a source of obligation and entitlement. People have to learn about their history before they can respond to it, but their education is no more an independent cause of their natural responses to injustice than the message communicated to the worker's family is an independent cause of its members' grief. Once we recognize that an automatic effect does not have to be proximate in time to its cause, there is no systematic way of ruling out as relevant to reparative justice psychological responses to injustices that occurred a long time ago.

Reconciliation and supersession

The common-sense view that historical entitlements and obligations fade away is wrong if that view is understood to require a statute of limitations on reparative claims. We cannot rule it out that a 600-year-old injustice could legitimately figure in a reparative claim. We cannot always suppose that more recent injustices are more salient than earlier ones. But this does not mean that the motivation behind common sense is mistaken. We rightly condemn those who undermine good relations by dwelling on ancient grievances or make it impossible for these relations to develop. A predisposition to overlook ancient injustices for the sake of maintaining respectful relations can be a healthy habit. Since the point of reparation is to bring about reconciliation, it is reasonable to assume that a recent history of respectful and just relations outweighs and supersedes injustices that occurred in the distant past.

Six hundred years ago Alpha and Beta were enemies and Alpha, being the stronger, committed many injustices against Beta, robbing it of some of its territory. The threat posed to both of them by the Deltan Empire eventually forced them to become allies, and for the last two centuries this relationship has brought both of them security and prosperity. They have come to trust and rely on each other. Nevertheless, the Betan Patriotic Front continues to complain about the perfidious Alphans, and demands from Alpha reparation for historical wrongs. From a common-sense, reconciliatory perspective we can reject the claim of this group. It is the subsequent history of a relationship that determines the significance of a past injustice and the existence of reparative entitlements, if any, and in this case subsequent history is positive. The Alphans have shown by their recent behaviour that they respect the integrity and interests of the Betan nation. The Betans can reasonably expect the Alphans to acknowledge in their official histories that the injustices were done. But the evils of the past have been superseded by recent historical developments.

We can, perhaps, reach the same conclusion about more difficult cases. Suppose that 600 years ago the Zetans drove the Xetans out of their territory and forced them to flee to a remote barren island, where they have eked out an existence ever since. Since that time the nations have had no contact with each other. The Xetans remain poor. On their island they have had none of the opportunities available to other nations to make themselves more prosperous. Not surprisingly, all Xetans remember the terrible wrong that was done to them so long ago. For them, it is as if it were yesterday, and they strongly believe that they are entitled to reparation. The Zetans, who had to cope with a more stimulating political environment, underwent during these 600 years wars, invasions, political revolutions and economic ups and downs. Their interaction with the Xetans is a minor, almost forgotten, chapter in their history books.

Common sense would judge, I assume, that the Xetans no longer have a legitimate claim to reparation. There could be a number of reasons for this conclusion. The Zetans have probably undergone political changes sufficient to disrupt the continuity on which responsibility depends. The Xetans might have been better off going somewhere else, rather than just sitting on their island nursing their grievances, and if they had, then presumably they would now have less to complain about. The responsibility for their condition rests at least in part on themselves. But the factor that seems most important from the reconciliatory point of view is that there is no reason to believe that the Zetans have retained through all this time the attitudes, interests or policies that caused them to commit the injustice. The Xetans should presume that a relationship can be established on a new basis, and that the past is irrelevant to their ability to establish such relations. Those who agree with this reasoning are affirming that opportunities to establish, as well as maintain, fair and trusting relationships should not be undermined by claims that have no connection with a recent history of injustice.

These examples suggest that the reconciliatory approach can account for our inclination to think that treaty obligations persist while denying that reparative entitlements have the same persistence. By fulfilling treaty obligations, we maintain respectful, harmonious relations – hence the presumption that they continue to exist unless there is good reason to the contrary. Whether reparative entitlements or obligations exist, on the other hand, depends on the present nature and more recent history of relationships between nations. Since respectful relations are the objective of reparation, entitlements cease to exist if such relations have come into existence or if there is no reason to suppose that they cannot exist.

A theory of reparation that focuses on repair of relationships provides as good a defence of common sense as it is likely to get. It does not favour digging up ancient grievances when they have been well buried under the sediments of more recent history. It will be predisposed to regard recent injustices as more salient than more ancient wrongs. If a nation has committed a number of independent injustices against another nation, then the more recent ones are likely to loom larger in the minds of members of the wronged nation. They are likely to have more of an effect on existing relations. In making his apology to the Irish, Blair may have reasoned that harms caused by the potato famine have more of an effect on Irish attitudes, and thus are more important for present relations between the British and the Irish, than more distant injustices. But of course recent injustices are not always more significant, and he may have been wrong.

Interpretations of history

I have argued that the salience of an injustice to requirements of reparation depends on its place in a history; but this in turn depends on how people interpret their past. One difficulty posed by my thesis is obvious, and has already been mentioned. Nations are prone to interpret history in their own favour and in ways that contradict the interpretations of their neighbours and rivals. Moreover, many philosophers insist that there is no such thing as an objective, neutral interpretation of history. So a theory of reparation that depends on people's interpretation of their history seems to invite irresolvable disputes about the meaning of historical events. The dangers are obvious, but unavoidable. Any theory that requires people to make value judgements about historical events and to assess their relation to present harms has to allow for debates about the meaning of history. But controversy in the context of an approach that aims at reconciliation is not an insuperable problem.

In the 1960s and 1970s, non-Maori people (Pakeha) of New Zealand generally believed that the problems in their history associated with race had been resolved. Most recognized that injustices had been committed against Maoris in the distant past, but assumed that these had been superseded by a more recent history of equality and amicable relations. New Zealand, they thought, was unusual in this respect, and they were proud of their accomplishment. So when Maoris began making demands for reparation for the violation of the Treaty of Waitangi, a common reaction among Pakeha was to complain that these demands were unfair and destructive of a good relationship. From the point of view of the Maoris, their relations with the Pakeha had never been just. The problem was not merely that Maoris were disadvantaged – that they were more likely than Pakeha to be poor, unemployed or in prison, or that they were sometimes the victims of discrimination. As they saw it, their present situation and the discrimination they sometimes faced could not be properly understood without reference to their history. Their relations with the Pakeha, as they saw them, were founded on injustice – on the lack of respect of the Pakeha for Maoris as a people, and a continual refusal to recognize entitlements that were supposed to have been protected by the Treaty of Waitangi. This old injustice remains salient to them, because they understand their history and their present situation as a continuation of a history of injustice that began with the violation of the treaty (or perhaps even earlier).

Whose interpretation of history is right? The lack of an objective, neutral narrative has not prevented progress from being made in the attempt to answer this question. The challenge that Maori activists posed to standard Pakeha accounts of history was the beginning of a dialogue which resulted in a more sophisticated understanding of that history. Historical evidence played an important role in this debate, as did reassessment of present relationships. In this case, as in many others, people are not likely to reach a common interpretation of the past. But lack of agreement is not fatal to reparation as reconciliation. Reconciliation can take place through discourse and debate so long as there is a commitment to finding a mutually acceptable resolution of disagreements about what, if anything, is owed.

6

All Things Considered

Territories claimed by members of dispossessed nations are now occupied by others. Another nation is in possession and makes the law of the land. Members of that nation own or lease the land in accordance with this law, and in some cases their families have been living on it for many generations. These people have built their homes on its soil, cultivated it, and have come to depend on its resources. If this land were to be given back to descendants of the dispossessed, present inhabitants would not necessarily be rendered homeless. Possession is different from private ownership. And in some cases all that dispossessed people demand, or can reasonably ask for, is access to their sacred sites (as I argued in chapter 4). However, change of possession is bound to affect the lives and economic circumstances of those who now live on lands subject to reparative claims, and if people of the dispossessed nation intend to make it their home – as presumably do the Sioux – this is likely to mean that some present inhabitants will have to give way. Even if they are able to stay, loss of land and restrictions imposed on their activities may make their farms and businesses unviable.

The fact that people of another nation now own and occupy land claimed by indigenous people and believe that they have a right to live on it and use it according to their laws means that these claims are causes of political and social conflict. In most countries where the issue has been faced, courts have generally ruled that freehold property is immune to the claims of indigenous people. For example, the ruling of the High Court of Australia on native title excluded property owned by individuals, companies or families from being the subject of native title claims.[1] Such land was assumed to be alienated for ever – not only immune to reoccupation by indigenous people, but outside the territory that they could claim as their national possession. However, the High Court allowed that land held by lease from the Crown (which includes much of 'outback' Australia) was not immune to claims. State and federal governments responded to this ruling by introducing legislation designed to put further limits on what could be claimed. In practice, the land that has been returned to indigenous people in most countries is usually land which no individuals or companies own or lease: state forests, national parks or other unoccupied areas in the public domain.

Judges are required to make rulings according to the law as it exists, and legislators respond to the pressure of their electorates. This makes it important to subject the debate over land to moral scrutiny. Do those who now occupy and use the land to which dispossessed people are entitled have any right to it at all? Is their entitlement, if it exists, stronger or weaker than the entitlement of the dispossessed? If present owners are forced to yield to the claims of the descendants of former possessors, then what, if anything, should be done about the losses they suffer? And what recompense should be given to the descendants of the dispossessed if they are the ones who have to yield?

These questions are not answered by the position that I have developed in the previous chapters. I have argued that a history of injustices can give people of a nation a moral entitlement to have returned to them the land of their ancestors. However, an entitlement is a right, all things being equal. It may be outweighed by the rights of others or considerations of other kinds. To come to a conclusion about what should be done, 'all things considered', we need to take a close look at the issues in debates about entitlements to land and resources.

Being pragmatic

The problem of determining who has the right of possession, all things considered, would have a simple solution if it turned out that present occupants have no entitlements at all. If, as Nozick supposes, those who possess a rightful title to property or territorial possession are either original possessors or those who received it through a legitimate exercise of the right of transfer, then those who occupy land unjustly taken from others are not rightful owners. A historical blemish, however far in the past, is a disqualification. But Nozick's views about acquisition, transfer and the persistence of title face serious difficulties (as I argued in chapter 4). Since virtually all titles are blemished, his theory, even if accepted, would probably not provide any more comfort to claimants than it does to present occupants.

There are, however, other, more plausible ideas about how titles are gained and lost. Jeremy Waldron favours the following account. A person who takes possession of something unowned by others, who works on it, shapes it and makes it part of her life, pivotal to her projects and plans for the future, has acquired a right to it. If it is unjustly taken from her, her plans and projects are seriously disrupted. She is entitled to have it returned to her. But if time passes, and she does not get it back, her right to it diminishes and eventually disappears. She has had to learn how to live without it. It is no longer central to her life plans. Meanwhile, it has become pivotal to the projects and plans of others, and Waldron's account suggests that these present possessors (at least if they are not themselves responsible for the injustice) have gained a title to it.[2]

Waldron uses this account to argue that land claims that stem from injustices of long ago are not likely to be valid.[3] However, in the cases being examined, we are dealing not merely with the property rights of individuals, but with the entitlements and obligations of nations, and this makes a critical difference. The United States is the present possessor of land once held by the Sioux, and present inhabitants are the national successors of those who did wrong. They, along with other members of their nation, have an obligation of reparation. Giving back some of the land once possessed by indigenous peoples is in many cases the form that reparation ought to take. So those who want to defend the entitlements of present inhabitants have to explain why their interests should prevail over the reparative entitlements of those who claim the land.

One set of arguments for maintaining the *status quo* appeals to the general good of the people of a society, or of world society as a whole. A change to the status of the land, it is often argued, would be economically disruptive – especially if present ways of using it play an important role in the national economy. 'We simply can't afford it' is a common response to reparative claims, and sometimes it may actually be true. In the international affairs of nation-states, appeals to the disruptive effects of attempts to fulfil moral requirements are especially common. When one nation unjustly invades another and takes over some or all of its territory (as China did in Tibet, and Indonesia in East Timor), and no nation or international body is able or willing to take immediate action, then, when the period for expressing their moral indignation is over, it is customary for leaders of nations to tacitly accept the existence of the new territorial boundaries. To do otherwise, most people reason, would be to invite war or other dire consequences.

These appeals to the potentially bad consequences of repairing injustices, whether recent or historical, can be interpreted in two ways: as arguments in the framework of an act-consequentialist or 'realist' ethics, or merely as examples of pragmatic reasoning.[4] Those who take the first course believe that the right thing to do in any circumstance is to bring about the greatest good (the act-consequentialist position), or to serve the best interests of one's state, economy, nation or party (as many realists insist). Those who act according to these principles believe that doing so is their only obligation; there are no opposing obligations or entitlements to consider. Someone who is being pragmatic about a particular issue does not deny that entitlements and obligations exist – that, for example, people ought to keep their promises, oppose injustice, and make reparation for the wrongs they have done – but she believes that doing so under the circumstances would have unacceptable consequences and that, all things considered, she is justified in ignoring her obligation.

The ethical position I have adopted in this study is neither act-consequentialist nor realist. It takes obligations and entitlements seriously, and in this respect reflects the ethical intuitions of most people. To the extent that my arguments are plausible, they confirm the correctness of this approach. It might be objected, however, that these arguments, and the ethical position that underpins them, are plausible only within a limited framework. Most of the cases I have discussed concern relations between indigenous and non-indigenous nations within a federal political society. In such a federation, the rule of law can prevail, and injustices can be punished and repaired. But outside the scope of this law is the arena in which states compete for power, riches and prestige. In international affairs the act-consequentialist or realist position seems to many people to be much more plausible.

However, few of those who regard themselves as realists about international affairs would deny that treaty making plays a crucial role in international relations. This means that they take seriously the moral requirements implicit in what the Vienna Convention refers to as 'good faith'. Most people are realistically pessimistic about bringing about justice in global affairs, but support it when there is a chance that it can be achieved. When the new government of Indonesia allowed the East Timorese to determine their own future after almost thirty years of Indonesian occupation, practical assistance and protection from Indonesians who wanted to sabotage the formation of an independent East Timor were provided by Australian and United Nations forces. Examples like this show that there is an idea of justice at work in international affairs, even though political actors are bound to have self-seeking motivations for their actions. Though not decisive, responses to such cases suggest that many people who think of themselves as realists are really pragmatists. They would like justice to prevail, but believe that in political affairs, especially in the international sphere, it is sometimes necessary for the sake of vital interests to break treaties, acquiesce in injustice, or ignore legitimate reparative claims.

Pragmatists have to convince us that the interests they want to protect are extremely important, not just to themselves but to people of their society or the world as a whole, and that fulfilling a moral obligation is likely to bring about consequences that are a serious threat to these interests. The greater the danger and the higher the probability that it will occur, the more convincing the pragmatist case. The conditions imposed on pragmatic argument are therefore likely to be easier to satisfy when issues of war and national security are at stake, but even in such cases the onus of proof falls on the pragmatists.

In cases where the entitlements of indigenous people are in question, the arguments offered by pragmatists are likely to be relatively weak. A reconciliatory approach to reparation demands that claimants take into account the present circumstances of those who owe them reparation. They are not entitled to make claims that threaten the existence of those others, or leave them with nowhere to go or no way to make a living. But if these restrictions on entitlements have been accepted, then pragmatists have little justification for ignoring reparative claims. They cannot suppose that the members of the nation that committed the wrong should be spared the necessity of making some sacrifices for the sake of fulfilling reparative obligations. Bad economic or political consequences of reparation may be a reason to postpone the fulfilment of obligations or to fulfil them over an extended period of time. What pragmatists are not likely to provide is a good case for ignoring the entitlements of indigenous people in favour of the interests of present occupiers and possessors.

Entitlements of occupants

Another attempt to defend the interests of present occupants draws on the justification for title offered by Waldron. Through their labour these people have established homes, farms and businesses which are now central to their well-being. Even if their government compensates them for their losses, they will be forced to give up activities and projects that have become central to their lives and their children's future. Moreover, many inhabitants claim that their attachment to their land is not merely economic, that they too have a spiritual tie to landmarks and places. 'The normal mountain person feels exactly about the land as the Aboriginal people do,' claims Leona Lovell. 'We don't own the mountains, they own us .... It's just a feeling that you belong to it.'[5] Does their attachment to their place, whether economic and spiritual, give present occupants an entitlement which their government should not violate even for the sake of fulfilling reparative responsibilities?

Let us assume that Waldron's account of how individuals acquire a legitimate title is correct, and that it applies to those who occupy land that was once possessed by indigenous people (even though this land was unjustly acquired by members of their nation). It is important to note that the entitlement which Waldron defends is not a right that we have to regard as fundamental and unassailable. Its existence and strength depend on the nature of the interests that are supposed to be protected – how important they are to the well-being or identity of individuals. So when there is a clash between the entitlements of members of a nation to reparation and the titles of individual property owners, then what should be done, all things considered, will in most cases depend on the relative strength of the entitlements – that is, on the relative importance of the interests that justify our belief that the entitlements exist.

Given that this is so, it seems that the entitlements of the non-indigenous inhabitants must be relatively weak. Governments often force people to sell their land or homes so that roads can be built, national parks proclaimed, and other public works undertaken. If it is justified to make people surrender their property for the sake of national projects, provided they are given adequate recompense, then it is surely justified to force people to surrender their houses or land so that their nation can make appropriate reparation. Since making reparation is a national undertaking, we would not expect these landholders to bear the burden alone. They ought to be compensated for their loss. The burden should be borne by all non-indigenous members of the society. Nevertheless, their entitlement to their possessions is less significant than the obligation of the nation, of which they are members, to ensure that reparative justice is done.

This argument is not by itself decisive. The right of a government to acquire land, even for important public purposes, has sometimes been questioned. However, it is difficult to suppose that the relation between a person and his property is so essential to his well-being that his rights cannot in some circumstances be justifiably curtailed or even removed. As a matter of fact, we do not generally believe that property owners who lose their entitlements are all that vulnerable to serious harm. This assumption lies behind beliefs about what governments are *not* required to do in order to ensure that people can keep their property. However central a piece of property becomes to an individual's life, he is not entitled to demand that his government protect him from all the contingencies that can sever the relation between him and his possessions. A government is expected to protect an owner from theft, and it may be expected to cushion him from economic loss; but it is not expected to ensure that he can in all circumstances retain the particular things that he owns. We may find it sad when a farmer has to give up his land because his business is no longer profitable, but few defenders of property would expect a government to give him the support he needs to keep his farm (unless doing so serves a social purpose).

How can we square a theory that justifies property rights by reference to the central role that possessions come to play in the lives of individuals with a cavalier disregard for the sad consequences of economic contingencies? I suggest it is because we assume that in a society that provides people with a range of opportunities, those who lose their property, either because of government policy or as a result of the slings and arrows of economic fortune, do not lose the ability to live a good life. They have access to other ways of making a living; they can often find ways of pursuing their projects in a different environment. Furthermore, they retain a secure membership in a society that confirms their sense of worth, and provides them with access to meaningful activities. In other words, the losses that they are forced to bear are not so devastating to their existence and well-being as individuals as to rule out from the start acquisition of their property for important public purposes – at least if they are fairly compensated for their sacrifice.

Reparation is an important public purpose, and when we have good reason to think that appropriate reparation should take the form of returning some of the land that was unjustly taken, then the entitlements of present owners should give way. Our reasons for thinking that reparation should take this form are sufficient to justify this result. This does not mean that the successors of dispossessed people will always have a right to the land of their ancestors. The Sioux in my imaginary history have no such right. The harms caused by a history of injustice have in their case been repaired. Nor does it mean that reparation always has to take the form of return of territory, rather than some other form of compensation.

Suppose that a hundred years ago Nation A unjustly invaded and took over a remote, sparsely inhabited part of Nation B's territory. Since that time A has put a lot of resources into the development of this area; many citizens of A now live there along with the descendants of citizens of B, who are treated as equal citizens. The people of B, though they are worse off as a result of losing some of their territory, do not lack other resources or the means to live meaningful lives; nor have they been oppressed or threatened in any other way by A. We might think that A still owes reparation to B, but even if this is so, it seems reasonable that it could take the form of compensation for loss of land and resources. The present harm to B which can be attributed to the injustice does not require anything more, and it would be unfair to demand back land which has by now become so central to the existence of members of A, and in which they have invested so much. If, on the other hand, A had used the territory it unjustly acquired to build a military base for threatening B, then our view about appropriate reparation will probably be different.

The theory in perspective

The argument of the first part of this study has now been completed. I have presented in the course of these six chapters a theory about the historical obligations and entitlements of members of nations. I do not deal with all cases or problems that arise when reparation and related matters are discussed. I assume, but do not attempt to show, that historical entitlements and obligations of corporations, churches and other politically organized intergenerational associations can be encompassed by the theory. I have concentrated on claims of indigenous communities and said less about the reparative demands made by nation-states, confining myself to a few remarks about how the theory applies to international debates about historical injustices. Even my discussion of the claims of indigenous communities is incomplete. I do not, for example, discuss the debate about whether indigenous people have a right to cultural relics or remains of their ancestors that are now held by museums or private collectors.[6] Though my presentation ignores many historical injustices and leaves out details that are likely to be important in discussions of particular cases, the theory I am defending is well enough developed to reveal its strengths – and also its deficiencies.

The philosophers and political theorists who have so far concerned themselves with reparative claims for historical injustices have left us with two unsatisfactory alternatives. We can adopt a theory that takes seriously the existence of historical titles and try to use it to defend some reparative claims. Or we can take a position similar to that advocated by Lyons and insist that entitlements of individuals depend on their existing needs, deserts or ability to contribute to the general good, and not on historical titles or injustices of the past.[7]

If we choose the first alternative, we are not only faced with the difficulty of justifying historical titles. We also have to defend entitlements that strike many as unfair. Why (as Waldron asks) should those who happened to be in a position to gain a title over a possession enjoy a right to resources that later comers cannot obtain? Why should some individuals have more wealth and opportunities than others, just because they are the heirs of those possessors? And why should individuals be able to make claims on resources just because their forebears were unjustly dispossessed? To people worried about social equity, Lyons's line seems much more attractive.

Concerning historical injustices, Lyons takes the view that all's well that ends well. But if all does not end well (as so often happens), then those who are disadvantaged by their history can make a claim on their society, but only for the relief of their disadvantages. Equity is all that matters. The case of the Sioux reveals the difficulties inherent in this position. Monetary compensation and provision of other resources seem to be all that the Sioux can reasonably demand in order to overcome their existing disadvantages. So those who think that the Sioux are entitled to the land of their ancestors either have to make a case for claiming that disadvantages of the kind suffered by the Sioux can be overcome only by a repossession of their homeland (which seems implausible given the adaptability often demonstrated by individuals and groups), or they have to allow that history should play more of a role in determining entitlements than a view like that of Lyons allows. I have argued for the latter.

The alternative I am presenting depends on two ideas. The first is that historical obligations and entitlements can be justified by attention to the implications of posterity-directed moral demands. Relationships between nations, the agreements they make, require us to make moral demands on our national successors, and thus to accept relevantly similar obligations arising from the actions of our predecessors. Historical agreements between nations as political agents are central to this account of historical obligation and entitlement – not historical acquisitions of title. The implications and presuppositions of these transgenerational agreements explain why we have historical obligations of reparation for the injustices committed against other nations by our predecessors.

The second idea is that the proper approach to reparative justice, at least in cases where injustices are historical, is obligations-based and reconciliatory. The existence of a historical entitlement depends on there being some agent who can be assigned the obligation of repair. The objective of reparative justice should be reconciliatory – a matter of bringing about just and respectful relations between successors of victims and successors of wrongdoers. Reparation requires that the perpetrators or their successors make recompense for harms that can be attributed to a history of injustices in such a way that this history does not stand in the way of achieving respectful relations between perpetrators and victims or their successors. Harms for which reparation is required include not just material losses, but psychological injuries and harms to relationships, and reparation as reconciliation will invariably involve acknowledgement of, and often apology for, wrongs done.

A reconciliatory approach to reparative justice provides support for the common-sense view that historical injustices can be superseded by more recent developments. And it makes possible a *rapprochement* between reparation and equity. It is respectful of the concerns of those whose objective is equity, while giving history its due. According to a reconciliatory approach, we are not obliged to restore the successors of the victims to the condition that members of their nation were in before the injustice occurred. We are responsible only for undoing or compensating for presently existing harms that can be attributed to the injustice. But this does not mean that satisfying the demands of reparative justice and applying the principles of equity amount to the same thing. Reparative obligations are incurred because of historical relations between nations. Just as nations can incur special obligations to each other by making an agreement – obligations that they do not owe to others – so reparative justice can give a nation special entitlements. To make reparation for breaking the Treaty of Waitangi and for other historical wrongs to Maoris, the New Zealand government is justified in extending to members of Maori communities privileges that other New Zealand citizens cannot claim. Even when reparative justice requires no more in compensation than could be claimed on grounds of equity, its demands can make a difference to how compensation is made and what else has to be done. Reparative justice always requires an acknowledgement of injustice, some act that makes it possible for members of the wronged nation to believe that those who have done them wrong are confronting their history and will henceforth treat them with respect. It may also require that compensation take a particular form. I have argued that the particular history of injustice suffered by the Sioux justifies their demand for the return of at least some of the land possessed by their ancestors.

Even when compensation for past injustice would give people of a nation nothing more and nothing different from what they could demand as their equitable share of resources, the fact that they are owed these resources in reparation for past injustices is likely to give their claim a priority over the demands of others suffering from the same kind of disadvantage. To demonstrate that they are now prepared to treat those they wronged with respect, members of nations ought to regard their reparative obligations as a matter of urgency.

The theory as it has been so far presented has obvious advantages, but also some obvious limitations. It not only insists that those who have historical obligations must be the members of organized associations like nations. It also seems to require that historical entitlements belong to people only in so far as they are members of such associations. This means that many reparative claims are beyond its scope. Not all of those who demand reparation for historical injustices are members of nations or comparable associations. Some indigenous people are no longer associated with the nation of their ancestors – their nation may have ceased to exist altogether – and yet it seems reasonable that these individuals should also be able to demand reparation for some historical injustices. Can it be fair that those lucky enough to be members of nations should receive compensation while those who are not miss out? Some reparative claims have nothing to do with injustices to nations. African Americans, for example, are making demands not as members of a nation, but as descendants of victims of injustice. The reasoning that I have employed in this part of my study cannot be used to justify their claims. In what follows I will argue that a theory with a similar focus – that is, one that emphasizes the moral importance of transgenerational relations – can be used to justify some of the reparative demands of descendants of victims.

PART II

Inheritance,
Reparation
and Family Lines

7

The Rights of Descendants

For many generations now, white children have inherited ill-gotten gains from the anti-black actions of whites before them. Recognition of this inheritance of privilege is the key to understanding arguments for reparations, and the key to bringing about reconciliation between blacks and whites.[1]

Reparation to black Americans should consist of a significant transfer of wealth, Joe R. Feagin and Eileen O'Brien conclude. Boxill agrees. 'Slaves had an indisputable right to the products of their labour,' and have presumably conferred their rights of ownership on their descendants. These descendants, he argues, are entitled to have this wealth returned to them by the wrongful possessors – the white community as a whole, who are the beneficiaries of the theft.[2] White society, says Randall Robinson, 'must, at long last, pay that debt in massive restitutions made to America's only involuntary members'.[3]

The demand for black reparations brings up some issues already discussed. It requires that members of nations take responsibility for what was done by their predecessors. It raises the question of what reparation should mean, and what form it should take, and whether relatively ancient injustices like slavery can still be the subject of reparative claims. But what makes the case of black reparations different from cases we have previously considered is that the people to whom reparation is supposed to be made are individuals – the descendants of the victims of injustice. They are supposed to be entitled to reparation not because they are members of a wronged nation. Their claims arise from the fact that their forebears were enslaved or suffered other kinds of injustice. This important difference is disguised by the fact that in law reparative claims are often defended as class actions of individuals who have suffered a similar wrong. But the fact that these individuals form a class does not make them representatives of a political community, and they are not claiming anything on behalf of such a community. If the US government were to pay reparations for slavery or other historical injustices done to blacks, it might decide to give the money to African-American associations, which would then be expected to use it for projects benefiting their communities. But it would do this for the sake of administrative convenience, or because it believed that this is the best way to ensure that the descendants of slaves will benefit – and not because these organizations are owed reparation. It made sense for the West German government to make payments to Israel in reparation for the slaughter, enslavement and persecution of Jews; not because it owed anything to this nation (which did not exist when the wrongs were done), but because Israel was in the position to ensure that many Holocaust survivors or their descendants would receive payments, and also because the symbolic purpose of the act would best be served by dealing with the nation that represented many Jewish people and was formed as a result of persecution of the Jews. (Germany also made payments to many individual Jews.)

The claim that the descendants of slaves are owed reparation for slavery or for other kinds of historical injustice done to their forebears is only one example of a kind of reparative claim that has become common in recent decades. The fall of communism in Russia and Eastern Europe brought with it demands for justice from those who had been victimized. Individuals who had been dispossessed, in some cases their descendants, demanded that property be returned, and most post-Communist governments have policies which allow limited recognition of these claims.[4] Japanese Americans and Japanese Canadians won from their governments reparation for forced internment during World War II, though descendants were excluded from these settlements. Victims of Nazi persecution, or in some cases their descendants, continue to make demands for the return of property or assets, or for recompense for forced labour.

Some problems

Reparative claims of people who have been dispossessed, enslaved or persecuted in an earlier part of their lives raise familiar legal and moral issues. Their claims may be difficult to substantiate in a court of law after so much time has passed. But, even if substantiated, they have to be weighed against the entitlements of people who now occupy or use property that was once unjustly seized. The legal compromises made by post-Communist governments in Eastern Europe between the rights of present occupants and the demands of the dispossessed are extremely controversial, and some insist that the rights of present occupants should take priority.[5] But difficulties of determining and weighing entitlements do not amount to reasons for denying to individuals a moral right to claim reparation for a wrong done to them at a previous stage of their life – especially if they have been prevented from making their claim at an earlier time.[6]

However, more serious problems arise when descendants claim reparation for injustices done to their forebears. In these cases the individuals to whom injustice was done are different from those who are now claiming reparation. It is a principle basic to reparative, as well as retributive, justice that obligations and entitlements associated with wrongdoing belong only to those who have done or suffered the wrong. Sarah cannot be recompensed for injury done to Sam. If Sam is beyond the reach of reparation, then no one is entitled to demand reparation for the wrong done to him. So how can individuals who have never been enslaved demand reparation for slavery or any other injustice suffered by their forebears?

One proposal is that they can claim reparation simply because they belong to the same group as their forebears. Enslavement and persecution, according to this idea, were visited on individuals because they were members of a group – because they were black Africans or their descendants – so it is reasonable that reparation for enslavement and persecution should go to current members of the group. This idea is reinforced by the fact that members of persecuted groups commonly develop a collective identity: members sympathize with each other's plight and often make common cause in struggling against persecution. A collection of persecuted people might even develop into an organized group capable of acting as an agent.[7]

From the fact that people can be persecuted just because they happen to belong to a particular group, it doesn't follow that these wrongs should be regarded as injustices done to their group. Individuals are the ones who are enslaved, denied opportunities, or discriminated against. The harm belongs to them. Even the suffering caused to members of the group because of the persecution of other members seems best understood as a harm visited on individuals. They are made to feel badly about harm done to other members of their group because of what this harm implies about how people like them are regarded and treated. But if this is right – if harms done to the group of blacks, women or homosexuals are really harms done to individuals because they are black, women or homosexuals – then there is no way of justifying the claim that a black person, a woman or a homosexual is owed reparation just because she belongs to the same group as individuals persecuted in the past.

Since they cannot make claims as members of a persecuted group, descendants of victims have to justify their reparative demands by demonstrating that the injustices done to their forebears have violated *their* rights or caused *them* unjustified harm. There are two ways in which they might do this. The first is to claim that they too have been wronged by the injustice – that the harmful effects they suffer constitute a wrong done to them. The second is to argue that their status as heirs of the victims gives them title to possessions wrongly taken from their forebears, or at least an entitlement to receive recompense for dispossession. Let us look at each of these strategies in turn.

Harm to descendants

Injustice can cast a long shadow. It harms not only its immediate victims. Descendants of these victims are likely to lack resources or opportunities that they would have had if the injustice had not been done, or to have been adversely affected in other ways by the suffering of their parents or grandparents, or by other more indirect social ramifications of the wrong. For example, some people believe that slavery is the root cause of many of the disadvantages that African Americans now suffer – the reason why they have not prospered like other groups of immigrants. Justice as equity might require the removal of the disadvantages of those adversely affected by history. Humanitarian feelings may motivate us to try to alleviate their suffering. The question is whether they are owed reparation for historical injustices.

Reparative claims that hinge on a causal relation between an injustice and harms to descendants face serious difficulties. One of these is that injustice not only affects how people fare; it can also determine what people there are. African Americans who presently exist would never have been born if their ancestors had not been abducted and forced into slavery. But it doesn't seem to make sense for a person to claim that she has been wronged by a historical injustice if she would not have existed at all if the injustice had not been done. George Sher deals with the problem by saying that descendants of victims of injustice ought to be restored to the level of well-being that a related group of persons would have had if the injustice had not been done.[8]

The descendants of slaves would presumably be compared with those who would have been the present descendants of these ancestors in a world where they had not been enslaved. The problem is that it is not merely impossible to determine the level of well-being of these possible descendants. Since many things would have happened to alternative family lines between then and now, it is difficult to understand how these possible people could be related in a relevant way to actual descendants.

Even if this difficulty were resolved, or simply set aside, a further problem awaits those who appeal to the causal relation between past injustice and present harms to justify claims of descendants. This difficulty is discussed, and also illustrated, in Boris Bittker's argument for black reparations.[9] Bittker thinks that it is not plausible for African Americans to demand reparation for slavery, because slavery, he says, is not the injustice responsible for the disadvantages they now suffer. After the Civil War, reforms in the southern states, he thinks, were bringing about a society in which former slaves could take their place as free and equal citizens. If these reforms had been allowed to continue, the harms caused by slavery would eventually have been undone. However, history did not follow this course. White supremists and conniving state governments brought the period of reform to an end, and introduced a system of oppression and segregation designed to keep black people in a dependent, powerless position. It is this system, Bittker argues, to which present (for him, early 1970s) disadvantages suffered by African Americans should be attributed.

However, once he allows that unrealized possibilities are relevant to attribution of harm, he cannot stop short of assigning it to present or recently discontinued policies of discrimination or segregation. The system of oppression adopted by southern states after the Civil War could have been discontinued by later generations or by earlier actions of the federal government. It may be unrealistic to suppose that these policies could have been reversed at any time. Nevertheless, there would have existed in the course of history opportunities for reform and undoing harm that were not taken. The laws and practices that were suppressing black Americans in the 1950s and 1960s, Bittker concludes, are the real cause of their poverty and other disadvantages. He ends by advocating compensation to individuals who have been directly harmed by segregation policies. Historical injustices like slavery or the actions of southern white politicians after the Civil War have dropped out of the picture as far as his defence of reparative justice for black Americans is concerned, and with them the idea that they are owed reparation as descendants of victims of injustice.

His argument can be understood as an application of Sher's strategy for discounting ancient injustices (discussed in chapter 5). The disadvantages suffered by presently existing black Americans, according to Sher's way of putting it, are not the 'automatic effects' of slavery, or for that matter of the introduction of the Jim Crow laws in southern states. The harmful effects on descendants should instead be attributed to more recent injustices – to those past or present injustices that have directly affected their lives, to the failure of governments to overcome the disadvantages they suffer. This treatment of demands for black reparations applies to other cases in which descendants of victims demand recompense for harms caused by an injustice done to their forebears. In all these cases the collapse of demands for reparation for historical injustices to demands for reparation for present or recent injustices seems inevitable once we acknowledge that present harms are properly attributed to recent acts or failures to act.

This refusal to regard slavery and other historical injustices as a legitimate focus for reparation claims invites a reply similar to the one I presented in chapter 5 to those who believe that Indian nations can no longer claim reparation for dispossession that took place a century or more in the past. Harms caused by injustice include psychological damage as well as loss of assets and opportunities. What happened to their ancestors matters to people; recalling the injustices done to their family or community can cause them distress. A history of injustices can be demoralizing, destructive of esteem, or the cause of depression. Why, then, can't supporters of black reparations insist that recent failures to do something about the disadvantages now suffered by African Americans are merely one part of a history of injustice that began with slavery, encompassed segregation policies of racist state governments, and included injustices perpetrated or condoned for generations by government officials? In the context of this history, according to the argument, ancient injustices are inseparable from existing wrongs, and no reparation can be adequate that fails to address ancient as well as more recent injustices.

The problem is that this reply is not so convincing in cases where individuals on their own behalf, and not as members of nations, demand reparation for injustices that were done to their forebears. Members of a nation are supposed to remember, and be motivated by, its transgenerational entitlements and obligations – including those incurred in an earlier part of its history. They are supposed to care about the injustices committed by their nation; they are entitled to be concerned about the injustices done to it, and how these are related to each other and to present harms. But the moral identity of an individual – what she is responsible for and what responsibilities others have to her – is surely confined to her actions and relations, and what others do to her. Her well-being and self-respect depend on how her contemporaries treat her and whether her society provides her with resources, treats her as an equal, extends to her the rights of citizenship, and protects her against wrongdoing. She can reasonably demand recompense for the wrong done to her by the failure of her nation to end discrimination or to combat a tradition of racist behaviour. But the fact that this wrong is part of a history of injustices which also wronged her forebears seems irrelevant to her case. It is true that recollection of a history of wrongs can cause people to suffer. Many of us care about what happened to our forebears or what they did. But what needs to be explained is why this harm gives anyone a right to reparation.

This way of treating the response of individuals to the history of their family or community may strike some people as overly 'individualist' – in the sense of the term MacIntyre uses when he criticizes the individualist self (see chapter 1). If the history of my family or people is woven into my account of who I am, then, according to MacIntyre, what my forebears did, or what was done to them, not only gives me emotions but also obligations and entitlements. My moral identity encompasses the history of my family or community. What wronged its past members also wrongs me. One trouble with this idea is that communal identities are by no means universal or have uniform implications. But the more serious issue is how we should regard the demands they encourage. Why should identifying with a community or family give people an entitlement to demand reparation for wrongs done to past members? Until this question is answered, we will not have a good case for making reparation to individuals for wrongs done to their forebears.

Inheritance

The second strategy for justifying reparative claims of descendants of victims of injustice is to derive their entitlement from their status as heirs. This approach looks more promising, because it makes entitlement depend on inheritance rather than on attribution of harm. The entitlement that individuals inherit is not strictly speaking an entitlement to reparation. The entitlement exists by virtue of their being heirs to possessions that would have been theirs if the injustice had not been done. By being deprived of their inheritance, they have been unjustly deprived of *their* right to possession. An approach to justification that appeals to inheritance not only allows individuals to make claims for reparation for historical injustices; it allows them to do so even if they have not been harmed in any other way than by being deprived of their inheritance. Moreover, it provides a way of getting around the problem caused by the fact that in many cases their existence depends on the injustice. The claims of descendants depend on them being the heirs of their forebears – not on their being the particular individuals that they are. The fact that they might not have existed if the injustice had not been done does not undermine their claim.[10]

However, an approach to reparation that appeals to inheritance also puts limits on what kinds of injustice can be the subject of claims. Claims have to be confined to demands for restoration of, or compensation for, expropriated possessions. Descendants can claim nothing in reparation for the murder, torture, abduction or maltreatment of their forebears, for the disrespect shown to them as persons, however large these injustices may loom in their thoughts about the past. Being robbed of the fruits of their labours is only one part, perhaps a small part, of the injustice done to the forebears of African Americans. This description of the wrong does not do justice to the injustice of slavery. Nevertheless, demands for reparation often involve claims for loss of possessions. So if these claims can be justified, this would be a good result for those who want to defend the reparative entitlements of descendants.

Right of bequest – that is, the right of a person to determine who shall inherit his possessions after his death – is recognized by virtually every legal system, though most put limitations on what goods or how much wealth can be transferred in this way. By recognizing a right of bequest, a society is committed to defending the right of heirs to receive their inheritance. But right of inheritance is not always conditional on right of bequest. Most societies adhere to Locke's principle that parents should be required to make provisions in their wills for their dependents.[11] In some societies – for example, those influenced by the Napoleonic Code – the law gives grown children a *right* to a portion of their parents' estate, and even in societies which allow individuals more freedom to dispose of their possessions as they please, spouses and children of the deceased are assumed to be the 'natural' heirs – those who are entitled to make claims on an estate and who are assumed to have a right of inheritance in the absence of a will designating otherwise. These legal assumptions have enabled descendants or relatives of Holocaust victims and victims of Communist governments to claim family possessions.

The fact that inheritance entitlements of various kinds are recognized by law does not mean that they can be morally justified.

A justification of the reparative claims of descendants calls for a defence of rights of property and inheritance, as well as a defence of their right to restitution. Property rights are themselves controversial, as we have seen. But even if we allow, in the manner described by Locke or Waldron, that individuals through use, cultivation, invention or discovery can acquire rights over things, the question remains what these rights should be. The right to make use of something during your lifetime does not entail a right to bequeath it to your children. Inheritance needs a justification – especially in a society which ensures that dependents will not lack resources – and many thinkers with socialist, left liberal or even capitalist convictions suspect that none can be found. Inheritance rights can be criticized from most of the moral perspectives that have dominated Western thought in the last 200 years.

They are questionable, first of all, from a consequentialist point of view – one that takes the maximization of well-being, or some other good, as the rightful objective of law and social policy. Those who inherit wealth are not necessarily the most efficient users of it, and their hold on resources hinders other people from reaching their productive potential and thus making a contribution to the welfare of their society. A consequentialist case against inheritance would have to take into account the positive effects that rights of bequest and inheritance are supposed to produce by encouraging people to work hard, invest and save for the sake of their descendants. An investigation of the effects of inheritance rights would have to determine how important, widespread and effective this motivation is. But even if it plays a positive role, its effects may not cancel out the bad, unproductive consequences of inheritance, especially if societies have other, and possibly more effective, means of encouraging hard work and investment.[12]

Allowing people to benefit from inheritance also goes against the principles of those who believe that people should be rewarded according to their deserts – for their skill, hard work, creativity and perseverance – in a society that ensures equality of opportunity. An equal opportunity society is supposed to find ways of overcoming inequalities that result from race, gender or family connections. Allowing inheritance to affect people's chances seems contrary to the very idea of a society where reward is supposed to be determined by hard work and talent, rather than by birth.[13] A defender of inheritance might point out that natural abilities or assets are just as beneficial to individuals, and no less unearned. Why should it be any more objectionable for a child to benefit from an inheritance than from being intelligent, artistically talented, physically attractive, or having a pleasing disposition? There is, however, an important difference between inherited wealth and natural assets. Natural assets have to be developed and put to work before they can be beneficial to an individual. A gifted person has to make an effort to obtain a reward. Those who inherit wealth get benefits without having to do anything at all.

Inheritance looks especially bad from an egalitarian point of view. Egalitarians who believe that the wealth of a society should be shared equally among its members, whatever their particular talents or contributions, are not likely to countenance inequalities that result from inherited wealth. Even those who are not committed to equality of outcomes harbour ideas about fairness that are in conflict with rights of inheritance. Fundamental to egalitarianism is the idea that assets which individuals obtain through accident of birth do not make them more deserving of social rewards. They do not justify inequalities. This idea underlies the thought experiment that John Rawls employs in *A Theory of Justice*.[14] Suppose, he says, that individuals who are rational and willing to co-operate, but are not inclined to put the interests of others above their self-interests, are set the task of determining the basic principles of justice for their society. The conditions under which they make their judgement – the requirements of the 'original position' – reflect what Rawls takes to be fundamental ideas about fairness. The agents make their decision behind a 'veil of ignorance', where no one knows his or her race, class, gender or religion, what abilities he has, or what kind of life he regards as good. Under these constraints, Rawls assumes that rational individuals, when considering how the basic resources of their society should be distributed, will allow only those inequalities that benefit everyone, particularly those in least well-off groups. This does not mean that inequalities that result from inheritance can't be justified. Indeed, Rawls claims (without much discussion) that they can. However, once the onus of justification is placed on those who want to maintain an inequality, inheritance rights are going to be difficult to justify – for reasons already explored. It will not be easy to establish that allowing inherited wealth provides greater benefits to the least well-off than would a system that does not allow this source of inequality.

Reparation and inheritance

This survey does not provide a decisive case against inheritance. Nevertheless, it shows that inheritance is more difficult to justify than many people suppose. And if inheritance is thrown into question, then so are the reparative demands of descendants who base their claims on right of inheritance. But even if we were able to justify inheritance, this would not overcome all of the difficulties faced by these claims. Let us assume that children are entitled to obtain bequests made by their parents – that an inheritance right of this kind is morally justified. Defending the right of inheritance, so understood, means protecting the right of people to make bequests and the right of heirs to receive them. But members of a society who recognize a right of inheritance are not necessarily committed to making sure that descendants obtain possessions that their parents or earlier forebears lost through an injustice. Common sense (and the law) assumes that the right of individuals or their descendants to reclaim what they lost is likely to disappear in the course of time.

Waldron argues (as we have seen in chapter 6) that considerations that justify ownership of property tell against the claims of descendants. Descendants cannot claim that the property owned and unjustly expropriated from their forebears plays a central role in their lives. Since this property now plays a central role in the lives of others (for example, those who are now living in the houses and farming the land once owned by people who fled from Communist regimes), it seems that they, and not the descendants of the victims of injustice, must have the stronger moral claim. I argued (in chapter 4) that the dependence of people on the resources, economic and spiritual, of their national territory gives their immediate descendants (like exiled Tibetans) a right to repossession. But this argument does not help descendants of victims of expropriation. If the nation to which these descendants belong provides them with sufficient resources and opportunities to live good, meaningful lives, then it seems that they have no injustice to complain of. If their society does not provide them with adequate resources, then (according to many views about justice) they can complain of inequity. But why should we suppose that they have a right to demand property that was taken from their forebears?

Waldron presents a further reason for doubting that descendants have such a right. To claim it, they have to be in a position to demand what they would have received from their forebears if the injustice had not been done. However, there is no way of establishing what this might be – if anything at all. The difficulty, he insists, is not merely epistemological – a matter of not knowing what these forebears would have bequeathed. Where human choice is involved, there is no fact of the matter. Even our best guesses about what people will do are often confounded. If victims of injustice had not been dispossessed, they might have disposed of their possessions in some other way. They might have gambled them away, made a bad investment, given them to someone else, or used them for their own projects. Even immediate descendants of victims have no right to assume that the property of their forebears would have been passed on to them if the injustice had not been done. The further the injustice recedes in time, the more choices that could have been made by intervening generations, the less credible this assumption.[15]

There are two ways of interpreting Waldron's indeterminacy thesis. According to the first, there is no answer to the question of what descendants would have got if the injustice had not been done, and thus nothing on which they can base their claims. Guesses, he says, have no moral authority.[16] The problem would apply as much to claims for restitution for more recent historical injustices as to more ancient ones – indeed, it is likely to apply to the demands of an individual for restitution for injustices done to him in an earlier part of his life. The second, more plausible interpretation allows that we can assert contrary to fact statements about human actions and choices on the basis of evidence, but insists that, as time passes and possibilities for choice multiply, our evidence becomes less conclusive. The issue then becomes one of onus of proof. Does it rest on those who make a claim for restitution, or on those who oppose the claim? Waldron seems to accept that it rests on those who make the claim, perhaps because of a reasonable concern about what he calls the 'contagion of injustice' – the ramifications over time of the effect of an injustice on people's lives, especially the lives of blameless third parties.

The difficulties discussed in this chapter put substantial moral barriers in the way of reparative claims of descendants of the victims of injustice. However, they are not likely to undermine a widespread conviction that descendants sometimes do have a right to reparation. Many people regard slavery as an episode in American history that cries out for some kind of reparation. Most of us are predisposed to believe that the heirs of Holocaust victims ought to have returned to them the works of art and other family possessions that were stolen by the Nazis – even when these are now in the hands of relatively blameless third parties. In the following chapters I will develop a perspective from which the two strategies for justifying reparative claims can be more successfully pursued. In chapter 8 I will defend a right of inheritance capable of justifying some reparative claims of descendants. In chapter 9 I will argue that individuals as members of family lines can plausibly claim that they have been wronged by injustices as ancient as slavery.

8

Inheritance, Equity and Reparation

'Inherited wealth', says Michael Levy, 'resembles a living fossil, curiously surviving the liberal egalitarian ethic of western societies.'[1] It is in tension, as we have seen, with major political philosophies of our time. But it also has it defenders. Consider, for example, the plea of Loren Lomasky:

> Confiscatory inheritance taxation runs roughshod over the deceased's interest in the ends his property will serve, substituting instead politically sanctioned ends to be advanced regardless of individual interest. It is an especially cruel injury because it deprives the dead of one of their last opportunities for securing the goods that they value. The dead can no longer offer loved ones their advice, their encouragement, sympathy in times of hardship, and joy when things go well; all they can do is pass on worldly goods to intended beneficiaries.[2]

This defence of inheritance implies that the interests of individuals survive their death, and indeed Lomasky insists that the dead have rights. Failure to respect bequests is a violation of the rights of individuals who have 'projects that assign value to states of affairs beyond their own conscious experience' and who care about the well-being of their descendants.[3] The idea that the dead have interests or rights is controversial, and, according to some people, untenable.[4] The dead have either ceased to exist as persons or they exist (according to the teachings of many religions) on a separate plane, where they are unaffected by earthly affairs, and nothing we can do will harm their interests. If they are nothing but ashes or mouldering corpses, it is difficult to see how they can have interests at all. But even if the dead have interests that can be harmed, they may not count for much. Aristotle thought that the effect of our actions on the dead must be 'weak and negligible'[5] – a description that suggests that harming their interests is not so serious a moral wrong as harming the interests of living people. The interests of the dead, even if they exist, may not prove a sufficient counterweight to considerations raised by opponents of rights of bequest and inheritance.

Nevertheless, Lomasky's defence introduces two considerations that seem important to an assessment of arguments concerning bequests, inheritance and reparation. The first is the fact that individuals often have projects and concerns that transcend their lifetimes. A political ethics that aims to promote the well-being or rights of living individuals needs to give these 'lifetime-transcending interests' their due. The second is that those who claim their inheritance or demand reparation for a lost inheritance are not merely individuals who might have received a property or been better off in a world where the injustice to their forebears had not been done. They are descendants of the victims of injustice. They have a special relation to these victims. I will argue in this chapter that these considerations, singly as well as jointly, not only provide a justification for bequest and inheritance, but can also be used to justify some reparative claims.

Lifetime-transcending interests

Most people, as Lomasky suggests, have interests that are 'lifetime-transcending'. They may be concerned about their posthumous reputation: about not being slandered or misrepresented after their death, or about being appropriately respected for their accomplishments or contributions. People often care about what happens to their bodies or bodily organs, about the disposal of their wealth or of possessions that have a special meaning to them. They are often concerned about the fate of their projects, or the survival of their values. They want the objectives they have worked for all their lives to be accomplished. They want their debts to be paid, their promises to be kept. They want the institutions that protect or make possible the activities that they value to be maintained. They want their nation or community to thrive. Most individuals also have a loving concern for the future well-being of their children, grandchildren and other people whom they care about. They want their descendants to live good lives; they may want them to live their lives in a particular way.[6]

Most of us have at least some of these interests, or we acquire them when we are forced to face the fact of our own mortality. But once we are dead, we will no longer be interested in our projects, values or offspring or care about our reputations or the way in which our bodies are treated. So why should the fact that we once had these interests put any restriction on the actions or policies of our survivors? This question can be answered, I think, without supposing that the dead have rights, or that their interests hang around like hungry spirits demanding satisfaction. The reasoning we need to employ is familiar from the arguments in the first part of this study. We are not only interested in things that will happen after our death. In some cases we think we are morally justified in demanding of our survivors that they respect, or do something about, these interests. But if we make these demands, or recognize that it would be legitimate for us to make them, then we commit ourselves to a moral practice that requires us to fulfil relevantly similar demands made by people who are now deceased.

Suppose you promise someone to pay them some money, and since you want to ensure that the person will get what you promised no matter what happens, you make an arrangement with a family member to fulfil your pledge if you die or become incapacitated. You think that your relative ought to honour his undertaking in the event of your death, not merely because a failure to do so is likely to harm the other person's interests, but because he has pledged to do so. By making this demand on him, you are subscribing to a moral practice that requires you (in similar cases) to keep the promises of the dead. If you fail to do so, you undermine a practice that you and others now living have a moral interest in maintaining. To recognize this failure as a moral offence, you don't have to suppose that you harm the dead by failing to keep promises that you made to them while alive.

The conclusion assumes that it is legitimate for people to impose moral requirements on their survivors. Some people believe as a matter of principle that they should not burden their successors with their requests: that their children and other survivors should be free to do as they please. A strict adherence to such a principle is likely to prove difficult. If there were no general agreement that contracts or promises of the dead should be kept, then, says Feinberg, 'there could be no confidence in promises regarding posthumous arrangements; no one would bother with wills or life insurance policies'.[7] This situation would be worse than inconvenient. To live good lives and fulfil their responsibilities to their children and other dependents, individuals need to make long-term, lifetime-encompassing plans. Since the pursuit of their activities, or the carrying out of their responsibilities, depends on co-operation of others, they have an interest, inseparable from their values, moral responsibilities and central concerns, in making long-term agreements and arrangements. Once these agreements come into existence, those with whom they are made are entitled to trust that they will be fulfilled, and 'posterity-directed' demands of the living, and the moral practices they give rise to, are measures for ensuring that their trust will not be violated due to death or incapacity. Practices that require the living to keep the promises and contracts of the dead are inseparable from the value we assign to the self-realization of individuals and their ability to fulfil their responsibilities to others.

Reasoning of a similar kind can be used to support what many people regard as an important duty to the dead: respecting posthumous reputations. The desire that our survivors protect our posthumous reputation is a lifetime-transcending concern that results from having other lifetime-transcending interests. There are two principle reasons why people with such interests might care about their posthumous reputations. First of all, they are likely be concerned about the harm that could be done after their death to their objectives, projects, values and the people they care about. Since slander can harm a person's family or community, or cause her works or ideals to become objects of ridicule, she will be predisposed to demand that her survivors not allow this to happen. Secondly, people are likely to want their efforts, accomplishments and objectives to be properly appreciated after their death by those whose opinion they respect and by the groups and institutions to which they have made a contribution. Having the respect of others is for most people central to a meaningful existence, and slander to a person's posthumous reputation would frustrate her desire for respect by making her labours or intentions objects of ridicule and disrespect.

Whether a person has one or both of these reasons for being concerned about her posthumous reputation, she will be justified in demanding that her survivors protect it from malicious lies and misrepresentations. If a person thought that her posthumous reputation would be vulnerable to people who would have no compunction about telling malicious lies for their own gratification or profit, she could not with confidence pursue lifetime-transcending interests or believe that what she did would make a contribution or be appreciated. This lack of confidence would seriously interfere with her ability and inclination to acquire and pursue lifetime-transcending interests. An important dimension of human activity and aspiration would be diminished. These considerations underlie the reasonable moral demand that our posthumous reputations be protected, and underwrite the practice of protecting them. Furthermore, they suggest that protecting posthumous reputations is an important moral requirement – one that should be central to any moral theory concerned with the ability of individuals to live meaningful lives. Not everyone cares about their posthumous reputation. Some people may have no interests that are threatened by what survivors could say or do. Some may even like the idea of being posthumously notorious. But even these individuals have a reason to accept a practice that requires them to respect the reputations of the dead. For if they are morally responsible people, they will have to acknowledge that others care deeply about how they are regarded after their death, and have reason to do so.

These considerations show that we do have duties in respect to interests once had by the dead (though not, strictly speaking, duties to the dead). This does not mean that *every* posterity-directed demand imposes moral obligations on survivors. A father who demands that his children live according to his values may have a deep interest in influencing their lives from beyond the grave. But most of us think that individuals should be free to choose their own values and way of life. This is, perhaps, the source of the common belief that people should not make demands on their survivors. The demand of the father is morally unreasonable – not one that we think his children ought to heed. More generally, the legitimacy of a posterity-directed demand depends on the nature of the interest behind it – on whether the values it serves are deserving of respect or compatible with other values we hold.

Individuals who make bequests to their children or other heirs are acting in the framework of a practice that requires their survivors to honour their wishes – at least in those cases where there is no good moral reason for not doing so. They are making posterity-directed demands on the people of their society. The issue in the debate about the rights of bequest and inheritance is whether these demands, and the practice that underwrites them, can be morally justified. I have shown, at least in outline, how some posterity-directed demands can be morally justified, and explained why others are not morally legitimate. How should we view demands concerning bequests and inheritance?

Inheritance and personal relationships

Lomasky offers two reasons in support of bequests and a right of inheritance predicated on right of bequest. The first is that a society ought to allow individuals to express their love and concern for their children and other loved ones through giving them gifts and bequests. Lomasky's emphasis is on individual freedom. He thinks that a society should respect the desire of individuals to act according to such strong preferences. But a defence of inheritance should also stress the importance to people (and to their society) of their being able to establish and maintain relationships which have as their natural expression the desire of participants to benefit each other, and which give rise to special duties of care and concern. Family members and friends are supposed to care about each other's well-being, to want to provide each other with services, to give each other benefits. Under some circumstances individuals believe that they have an obligation to promote the good of a family member or a friend. Given the important role that family and friendships play in most people's lives, given the role they play in social life, it is surely reasonable to think that a society ought to allow and support a practice that enables members of families or friends to give each other gifts – including gifts by bequest. The lifetime-transcending interest we have in the well-being of our family and friends predisposes us to accept and defend this practice.

These considerations show that there is a good case for favouring rights of bequest and inheritance. But we also have to deal with arguments against recognizing such rights. Natural though it is for members of families or friends to favour each other, their inclinations sometimes have to be curbed for the good of society and other individuals. People in public positions may be tempted to extend benefits or opportunities to their family and friends that they do not provide to strangers, but it would be wrong of them to do so, and we think they ought to be prevented from expressing their loving concern in this way. Those who oppose inheritance are arguing that we have reasons just as strong for restricting or preventing expressions of love and concern that take the form of gifts or bequests.

Using a public office to favour relatives and friends is wrong because it violates the presumption that every citizen has equal standing before the law and within public institutions. Willing your property to your child is not so obviously a misdemeanour. It is true that your child is being rewarded because of her relation to you and not her merits, and some economic inefficiency may result. Your property might be more productive in other hands. But you can surely justify your action by pointing out that the most significant relations between individuals are not economic and do not depend on merit. It is a good thing for children that their parents love them with a generous and even unconditional love. In the best of friendships individuals love each other for what they are, without considering whether their friends are really intelligent, beautiful or economically productive enough to be worth all the time and attention. A society that takes human well-being as its object should allow for and encourage such relations, and the fact that expressions of love and friendship may sometimes offend against meritocratic or consequentialist objectives is no objection to them.

However, inheritance and the giving of substantial gifts to children or friends can offend in a serious way against the principle that opportunities in a society should be equal or against egalitarian ideas about wealth distribution. Haslett points out that between 1 and 2 per cent of American families own between from 20 and 30 per cent of the net family wealth in the United States; and that between 5 and 10 per cent own from around 40 to 60 per cent. This concentration of wealth was achieved and is maintained through inheritance.[8] The situation is probably not much different in many other countries. Nevertheless, what makes this state of affairs morally questionable is not that parents pass on their wealth to their children, but the fact that they have so much more than their fair share to pass on. High inheritance and gift taxes may be a good way of redistributing wealth (though there are other causes of inequality that such taxes do not touch). But an insistence that inheritance be taxed is not the same as saying that it should be effectively abolished. In fact, few opponents of inheritance want to impose a total ban on gift giving. Haslett, for example, allows that individuals should be able to give each other small, insignificant gifts, as is common at Christmas or birthdays, and thinks that gifts that are quickly consumed are more acceptable, morally speaking, than gifts that can be used to increase wealth.[9]

In some cases Haslett's suggested limitations on gifts would be too restrictive. Suppose you live in an egalitarian society where no one is very rich and no one is poor. However, you save all the money you can and use it to buy beautiful things for your daughter – precious jewellery, silver cutlery, expensive china, etc. Your idea is that she will be able to enjoy an elegant life-style when she has a home of her own. Other people spend their money on entertainment and holidays. You put the money away for your child. It seems to me that no tax laws should prevent you from doing this, even though the gifts to your daughter are substantial. Of course, if she uses them as security on a loan to start a profitable business, then she will pay taxes to the extent required by the principles of justice in her society (for example, what is needed to satisfy Rawls's difference principle). But if she uses the gifts as you intend, to decorate her house and person, then it does not seem right to penalize her. It is true that not everyone has the chance to wear expensive jewellery or eat off elegant crockery. But this does not violate the principle of equal opportunity as most people understand it. Nor does her enjoyment of an elegant life-style prevent others from having good, meaningful lives.

There are bound to be differences of opinion about what people should be able to inherit or receive as gifts, whether there should be inheritance taxes, what should be taxed, and how high taxes should be. But the important point is that a society should allow people to express love and friendship by giving each other gifts, even gifts of considerable value. Taxes on gifts of value – at least, gifts that add to the income of the recipients – may be permissible for the sake of equity. But it would be wrong to impose taxes or restrictions that would undermine the practice of giving gifts or making sacrifices for the sake of children or friends. Our predisposition to believe that our survivors ought to honour our bequests can be morally justified (at least within the limits allowed by considerations of equity).

Inheritance and lifetime-transcending interests

There is a second reason for recognizing rights of bequest and inheritance which Lomasky particularly stresses. Individuals often labour not just for themselves, but for their community or family, for the sake of their ideals, or to make a mark on the world. Many will have a lifetime-transcending interest in how the fruits of their labour will be used or regarded. They cannot reasonably demand that their successors complete their projects, celebrate their contributions, or use the fruits of their labour in a particular way. Their successors will have their own projects to pursue and their lives to lead. But they can reasonably demand that they be permitted to pass on their projects or the results of their lifetime activities to those who are most likely to carry them on or appreciate them. A person who has put a lot of effort into amassing a small collection of expensive jewellery may want to pass it on to her children, who have been taught to appreciate it. Parents who have built up a small family business may want their children to have a chance to continue it. An artist may regard it as important to give her paintings to friends who truly appreciate them. A person who has spent most of his life running a literary magazine may want to bequeath it to someone who shares his philosophy. Given the importance to people of their lifetime-transcending interests, it seems reasonable that a society should not prevent people from passing on their projects, or objects they have invested with meaning, from one generation to the next. The recipients of the gifts are free to prefer their own projects and possessions, but at least they should have the chance to obtain what their predecessors intended them to have.

However, allowing individuals the opportunity to hand on their projects to their successors seems to offend against equal opportunity and equity. A newspaper mogul who owns media outlets all over the world may want to pass on his empire to an heir who will continue his policies. A wealthy rancher who owns most of the land in a county may have dynastic ambitions. If it is wrong for families to be allowed to perpetuate their wealth and power to the detriment of opportunities and freedoms others, then surely individuals cannot be free to pass on projects to their successors just because they have a lifetime-transcending interest in doing so.

This, of course, is true. But it does not mean that people should be blocked altogether from handing on to their heirs projects or things they have invested with meaning. Once again, it should be pointed out that those who blame this practice for social inequities are focusing on the wrong thing. It is not wrong of the newspaper proprietor or the rancher to think that he should be able to hand over something of what he has accomplished during his life to those who are likely to continue his project. What is wrong (if anything) is that some people have been allowed to acquire or retain so much wealth and power in the first place. High inheritance taxes may be a justifiable means of achieving greater equity, but a government should not aim to make it impossible for people to find meaning in their life by working on something that they can bequeath to those who are likely to appreciate their efforts or carry on their projects.

A society with egalitarian, utilitarian or meritocratic goals will put limits on what can be inherited, just as it is likely to put limits on what or how much can be privately owned or how property can be used. It may put restrictions on how people can use the gifts they are given. If a famous artist gives me a valuable painting as an act of friendship, it would be wrong for the government to force me to pay high taxes in order to keep and enjoy the gift. But if I use the painting for financial gain, then it seems more reasonable that my earnings should attract a high rate of tax. A government may in some circumstances have to restrict transgenerational transfers that are normally legitimate. It seems reasonable that farmers should be able to pass on their family farms to their children. But if no one else is able to become a farmer because all the land is controlled by family dynasties, or if these family farms over the generation have become large and powerful corporate enterprises, or if they are standing in the way of important agricultural reforms, then there is reason for society to intervene. The tension between important objectives of modern political philosophies and rights of bequest and inheritance cannot be entirely transcended, but this does not mean that these rights are fossils from an aristocratic or feudal past. Their justification makes reference to interests and values which these modern philosophies also acknowledge: the desire of individuals to live meaningful lives, to pursue projects that will be appreciated by their survivors, and to express their love and concern for particular others, especially their descendants.

I have argued that rights of bequest and inheritance can be justified – though not without restrictions and not necessarily without imposition of taxes. But given that these rights exist, however restricted, an individual is entitled to demand of his successors – that is, the people of his nation who survive him – that they honour his bequests and protect the right of his heirs to receive the inheritance to which they are entitled. In making this demand, he acquires a corresponding duty to uphold and respect the practice that ensures that the legitimate bequests of his predecessors are also honoured. It remains to be seen whether the rights I have defended enable descendants or other heirs of victims of injustice to make legitimate reparative claims – and if so, how long such entitlements endure.

Reparation and supersession

Justifications for inheritance that appeal to the value of personal relations or the interests of individuals in their projects and relations are able to allay Waldron's doubts about the reparative claims of descendants of victims of injustice. They allow us, first of all, to resist the contention that descendants of victims have no claim to something that is not part of their lives. Heirs who are prevented from receiving their inheritance must, as Waldron says, learn to live without it. They may not even miss what they never had. But this does not make their failure to receive it any less unjust. For the fact remains that they are being prevented from enjoying or learning to appreciate something that their parents or grandparents out of love and concern, or because of their own values and projects, wanted them to possess, and should have been able to bequeath them. A legitimate expression of love and concern, or a legitimate attempt to hand over a project or a treasured belonging to a successor, has been unjustly thwarted. Justice demands that such wrongs be rectified, all things being equal.

The approach I am defending is also able to resist Waldron's contention that the reparative claims of descendants are undermined because there is no way of saying what they would have received if the injustice had not been done. His argument, I have suggested, is best understood as a view about where the burden of proof belongs. The considerations I have advanced give us reason to shift this burden from those who defend reparative claims to those who oppose them. Entitlements that result from expressions of love and concern intrinsic to family relationships or friendships ought to be regarded with considerable respect. The desire of an individual to hand over a project or something they treasure to someone who might appreciate it is a desire to give meaning to the future-directed activities of a life. A society that protects and promotes such relations and activities ought to give the claims of heirs the benefit of the doubt.

Suppose parents work very hard to develop a small property that they want to bequeath to their children. This property is unjustly taken from them by a dictatorial political regime, and, because of their political circumstances, they are unable to claim it back during their lifetimes. Long after their deaths the political climate changes, and the children are in a position to make a claim. If the parents had retained the property, they might not have ended up giving it to their children. They might have gambled it away or sold it (as Waldron reminds us). They might have lost it for economic reasons. But so long as there is reason to believe that the property was intended for the children – and family relations make this assumption plausible in most cases – the children's claim should be regarded as legitimate. Should we so generously assume that the descendants of the victims would have been favoured by fortune if the injustice had not occurred? Those whose forebears were not done an injustice are forced to bear the consequences of outrageous fortune – of fires that destroy treasured possessions, parents who make unwise investments. But giving descendants of victims of injustice the benefit of the doubt is the right way to respond to their claims. It would be mean-minded to question the claims of descendants of Nazi victims on the grounds that their parents or grandparents might have lost their possessions in some other way if the Nazis had not stolen them. The generous response is more appropriate so long as we regard family connections, and other relations which encourage care and concern, as being something that a society ought to protect, or so long as we respect the desire of people to make their lives meaningful by handing on to others their projects or treasures. The importance of doing something to alleviate an injustice that is destructive of attempts by individuals to live meaningful lives outweighs quibbles about contingencies.

The same consideration supports the view that claims of descendants of victims will in many cases outweigh the claims of those who now possess things that were unjustly taken – even if these present possessors are entirely blameless. A society ought to defend the right of heirs to receive gifts that their parents or friends wanted to bestow on them (and had the right to bestow) – even when doing so imposes burdens on blameless people. What these heirs can reasonably demand depends, to be sure, on other considerations – including the importance of the thing in question to the lives of the people who now possess it. How a society should handle conflicting claims depends on its principles of justice and the situation of the people concerned. But upholding the values on which inheritance depends does suggest that even in an egalitarian society heirs should be able to obtain some part of what their parents or friends wanted them to have.[10] Such a society would reject the claim of the heirs of a dispossessed aristocrat to his vast estates in pre-Communist Eastern Europe. But it would uphold their right to receive possessions (or some part of the possessions) that their parents especially treasured and wanted them to have.

However, the rights of bequest and inheritance that I have defended so far do not advance the case of many of those who make reparative claims. Nor do my arguments meet Waldron's main concern, and the point of his insistence on supersession, which is to eliminate from consideration reparation claims that stem from less recent injustices – injustices that took place more than one or two generations ago. My defence of inheritance, as I have developed it so far, does not support claims of distant descendants to the possessions of victims of injustices. Indeed, it suggests reasons why their claims should not be taken seriously.

Gifts are given to particular loved ones. Projects or treasured possessions are handed on to those who may value them. These recipients have a legitimate claim to what was meant for them. But the plausibility of their claim depends on their having had a personal relation to the deceased, or at least being someone who was known to the deceased. Since distant descendants cannot claim such a relation, their reparative demands are open to doubt. A child might suppose that his mother would have passed on a gift which her grandfather would have given her if he had not been dispossessed. But there are good reasons for doubting this contrary to fact claim. The gift that the grandfather wanted to give to his granddaughter would have been hers to do with as she pleased, and if she had received it, she might have sold it or used it for her own projects. What she would have given to her child as his inheritance would have depended on her relation to him, and what she regarded as his needs or interests. Because his claim is open to doubt, he bears the onus of proving that he has a claim on the possession.

It is not always true, however, that distant descendants can make no plausible inheritance claims. We generally assume that possessions that belong to a family – family heirlooms are obvious examples – can be claimed by individuals simply because they are members of that family, and not because of any personal relationship between the member who first acquired the possession, or had it stolen from him, and the recipient. If, according to family custom, the oldest daughter gets the family jewels, then I as the oldest daughter am entitled to claim them simply because I have that position in my family. Possessions that belong to the family side-step the problem of contingency discussed by Waldron, and can give rise to claims that are not easily superseded. If I am entitled to get the family jewels by virtue of my position in the family, then this entitlement exists whether my mother wants to give them to me or not. If she decides to favour my sister or to sell them, I can complain that I have not received my rightful inheritance. If they do rightly belong to me, then I can claim them whatever the contingencies of choice and fate. I can claim them even though I had no personal relationships with the person who acquired them, and if someone stole the jewels from our family several generations ago, then surely the burden of proof rests on those who wish to deny my claim. I can side-step the problem posed by Waldron because my inheritance entitlement does not depend on someone else's right to exercise their freedom of bequest. I am appealing to the 'unconditional' right of inheritance that most systems of law recognize in some domains to protect the rights of dependents, or to underwrite responsibilities that members of families are supposed to have to each other.

When family heirlooms are in question, we find it reasonable to assume that individuals have a reparative entitlement simply by virtue of their membership or position in a family. But the fact that claimants are members of families – descendants or relatives of victims of injustice – makes a difference in other contexts. We assume that children or relatives have a claim to the possessions of Holocaust victims, even in the absence of any indication that the victims would have wanted family members to have these things. We assume, in the absence of any reason to believe the contrary, that children and spouses are the rightful heirs of the deceased. Victims of injustice might have given away or sold their possessions if the injustice had not been done. But nevertheless, we tend to assume that their descendants are entitled to make a reparative claim. Contrary to what Waldron supposes, we generally give them the benefit of the doubt. To understand why this is so, and what it means for attempts to justify reparative claims, we have to consider why families and family relationships are accorded so much respect.

Justice and family lines

Rawls maintains that those who determine principles of justice for their society could be thought of not simply as individuals, but as 'representatives of family lines'.

> The parties are thought of as representing continuing lines of claims, as being so to speak deputies for a kind of everlasting moral agent or institution. They need not take into account its entire life span in perpetuity, but their goodwill stretches over at least two generations.[11]

These contractors, so conceived, are not individuals concerned only with their own interests. They are representatives; they are assumed to care about their families. A theory of justice, Rawls is implying, is not satisfactory unless it can be endorsed from this perspective.[12] If we can appreciate the reasons for giving representatives of families such a prominent role, we will be in a better position to justify the respect for family lines implicit in law and our intuitions about inheritance and reparation.

Rawls has an obvious reason for introducing these representatives. A theory of justice for an intergenerational society must encompass relations between generations as well as relations between contemporaries. Rawls makes use of representatives of family lines to determine what obligations members of a society have to future generations. Because these 'fathers of families' care about their children and grandchildren, they will be predisposed to accept a collective obligation to save and pass on resources to their descendants.[13] Rawls is grounding an unconditional right of inheritance possessed by individuals in virtue of their status as members of a political society – one that imposes an obligation on their forebears to provide them with a fair share of socially created resources.

Nevertheless, giving preference to the point of view of those who represent families seems to offend against a precept accepted by Rawls and most other liberal theorists: that a state, in its policies and principles, should not favour any particular ideas of the good. It should not assign special privileges to people who subscribe to a particular religion or believe in a particular ideal. Families are central to the lives of many people. Most people care about their children and assume they have responsibilities to them. Rawls's use of this perspective may reflect the fact that people are not likely to regard principles or institutions as just unless they are at least compatible with their family concerns and responsibilities. However, not everyone cares about family life or has children. Why should childless people without family ties accept principles determined by representatives of family lines? There are several, closely related answers to this question.

In existing societies, the family plays a central role in the psychological and moral development of individuals. The family has the primary responsibility for constructing our identities and giving us a place in a history that began before our birth and to which we relate the events of our life. To the family is also given most of the responsibility for forming individuals capable of being autonomous selves and good citizens – people who are able to appreciate and perpetuate institutions of justice.[14]

One of the important and valuable aspects of family relations – one that Rawls depends on in his reasoning about future generations – is that they are transgenerational. Parents take responsibility for raising their children. They induct them into a culture, a community and a political society, and are responsible for giving them a foundation that will enable them to become individuals with a sense of justice. Parents are supposed to be concerned for their children's well-being and, by being concerned, provide them with an environment in which they can grow into self-confident, thriving adults. This parental concern and sense of responsibility is likely to remain, in a modified form, even when their children are grown, and to extend to their grandchildren. They want their children to be in a good position to raise *their* children; they want their grandchildren to have good lives. And most grown children think that they have some degree of responsibility for their ageing parents, even if they are not required to give them financial support. Family relations, when they work well, not only produce good citizens; they also ensure that people get, without much need for state intervention, the personal concern and support that they need in the various stages of their life, and that at least some of their lifetime-transcending desires will be fulfilled.

So it is reasonable to regard family relations, especially the transgenerational bonds of concern and responsibility that are central to them, as something that a society ought to protect and promote. The functional role of the family in a just society gives even those who do not have children, or who do not care about their family, a reason for endorsing principles, laws and institutions that give due regard to family relations. This does not mean that we have to endorse or approve of families as they now exist. Nor do we have to suppose that the proper representatives of family lines are fathers of families, as Rawls and most others in the liberal tradition have assumed. But we do have to assume the value of loving, responsible and authoritative relations between adults and children that perpetuate themselves through the generations. It is possible to imagine ways of raising children that don't involve families in any form: bringing up children in institutions run by the state, for example. But it is difficult to suppose that these alternatives could adequately perform the functions that families are supposed to fulfil. In any case, they would not be accepted by most people, who do, as a matter of fact, regard their relationships with their children as valuable, and think that they ought to care for them and provide for their future well-being.

With these considerations in mind, we can provide more weighty reasons for endorsing and protecting rights of bequest and inheritance, and for giving reparative claims of descendants of victims the benefit of the doubt. Those to whom individuals hand on their projects or the things they love may not be their children or grandchildren. But in most cases the people who are most likely to remember the deeds of the dead, or care about what they accomplished, are members of their family. People often want to express their love and concern for their friends and partners by giving them gifts. But their concern for their offspring is not merely a matter of love. The provisions they make for their children are often motivated by a feeling of responsibility for their well-being and happiness. In a society where individuals have an equal opportunity to obtain positions and wealth, parental responsibility largely ends when children are grown. But few parents think that it ceases entirely, and most regard themselves as having an obligation to help their grown children in time of need, or to do what they can to ensure that their grandchildren will have a good life. They are, after all, the ones who are intimately acquainted with the needs and interests of their children, and bear some responsibility for the way their desires were formed. These considerations give us good grounds for assuming that the heirs of victims of injustice are their children or grandchildren unless we have reason to think otherwise. The nature of family relations, and the reasons citizens have for supporting them, underwrite our inclination to look with favour on the reparative claims of descendants of victims of injustice.

To have a reparative entitlement, it is not necessary that descendants had a personal relationship with their forebears. The fact that they are descendants of the victims could be a sufficient basis for making a legitimate claim. This is obviously true when family heirlooms are in question. Moreover, we allow that parents can care about, and make provision for, the well-being of potential grandchildren even if they never have a chance to become acquainted with their children's children. Nevertheless, the question remains: how far down the generations does the entitlement to reparation extend? Rawls thinks that the just savings principle encompasses two generations –

children and grandchildren. He assumes that the responsibility of representatives of family lines stretches only that far. The justification I have offered for the entitlements of descendants of victims of injustice suggests that they are similarly limited, at least in the case of bequests. Parents mean to express their love or connection to their children or grandchildren, and think that their society ought to ensure that these individuals obtain their inheritance. They are not likely to be unduly disturbed by the possibility that their distant descendants may fail to receive these things (at least in a society where individuals are not likely to be disadvantaged by injustices that happened many generations ago).

Family heirlooms are another matter. They belong to families, not to particular individuals, so if they have been passed down from one generation to another for a very long time, and have become important to family history or tradition, then descendants are likely to have a claim on them even if more than two generations have passed since the injustice was done.[15] However, family relations change, connections between existing people and distant generations become tenuous, and ideas about what is meaningful to the family do not stay the same. So, as time passes, even these claims will become less plausible. In the last analysis, Waldron is surely right: injustice is superseded by the passage of time.

If this is so, then my defence of the right of inheritance is unlikely to support the claims of descendants of African slaves for the fruits of the labour of their ancestors. There are other considerations which pose a problem for these claims. To claim a lost inheritance, descendants must be able to specify what possessions they should have received from their forebears. They must be able to establish that they are the ones entitled to make a claim. In most cases descendants of slaves will not be able to satisfy these conditions, either because there is no way of establishing what possessions their forebears had, or would have had if they had not been enslaved, or because there is no way of determining who their slave forebears were. If black Americans are going to be able to claim reparations for slavery, it must be on grounds other than right of inheritance.

9

Reparation and Injustices to Family Lines

Like slavery, other human rights crimes have resulted in the loss of millions of lives. But only slavery, with its sadistic patience, asphyxiated memory, and smothered cultures, has hulled empty a whole race of people with transgenerational efficiency. Every artifact of the victims' past cultures, every custom, every ritual, every god, every language, every trace element of a people's whole hereditary identity, wrenched from them and ground into a sharp choking dust.[1]

In one way or another, Randall Robinson implies, all presently existing African Americans are victims of a history of injustices that stem from what he calls 'the most heinous human rights crime visited upon any group of people in the world over the last five hundred years'.[2] Yet, for reasons already discussed, black Americans as individuals cannot claim reparation for slavery or other wrongs done to their ancestors. Reparative entitlements of individuals arise only from wrongs done to *them*. Nor can black Americans claim reparation because they are members of a racial group whose members were wronged in the past. Black Americans as a group do not constitute an agent to whom wrongs can be done. Nevertheless, Robinson's insistence that the American nation has incurred a debt to black Americans because of slavery and other historical wrongs is difficult to dismiss. Can this idea be defended?

Harms that can be traced back to slavery are passed down through family lines. Slavery harmed and, through its effects, continues to harm families. Does this mean that individuals can claim reparation as members of families? Can their reparative claims be justified in the same way as the claims of members of nations are justified? This suggestion, at first glance, seems no more promising than the idea that individuals have reparative entitlements by virtue of being members of a racial group. Families, at least in modern Western societies, are not organized groups. Unlike nations, they do not act as agents, and do not incur the obligations and entitlements that belong to agents.

Families, unlike nations, do not have obligations of this kind. But being part of an organized group like a nation or a corporation is not a necessary condition for having entitlements based on membership. As I argued in the last chapter, individuals sometimes have reparative entitlements by virtue of being members of families – for example, by having a rightful claim to family heirlooms or other property presumed to be inherited through family lines. These possessions, it could be said, belong to the family, and unjust expropriation is not merely a wrong done to the individuals from whom they were taken. It is a wrong committed against the family, or the family line to which forebears and their descendants belong, and present members are entitled to make a reparative claim simply because they are family members, or members with a particular family status.

In this chapter I will develop this idea further. I will argue that there is a category of wrongs properly described as 'injustices to family lines', that they include crimes more serious than stealing family heirlooms, and that present members of families can claim reparation for at least some of these injustices. One of my aims is to establish that slavery, at least as it was practised in the American South, was an injustice to family lines, and that descendants of slaves can claim reparation for slavery (as well as more recent injustices) as a wrong committed against their family lines. However, to introduce the notion of an injustice to family lines, I will focus on an injustice from a different time and place.

Injustice and the removal of children

As documented by a report of the Australian Human Rights and Equal Opportunity Commission, Australian state governments, from the beginning of the twentieth century up to recent times, pursued a policy of removing half-caste children from their Aboriginal families and putting them into orphanages or white foster families.[3] For many years legislation allowed children to be removed without the consent of their parents. They were simply abducted from Aboriginal camps or homes and transported to a distant location, and attempts by family members to visit or communicate with them were systematically thwarted. Though in later years removal of children depended on the agreement of the parents, consent was often obtained by coercion, and parents were given misleading information about where their children were being taken and how long they would be away. Many of the removed children never saw their families again, some not for twenty or more years, and had by this time lost the ability or inclination to participate in the life of their kin or community. The policy of removal was visited on Aboriginal families generation after generation, and many of those who were taken away as children had their own children removed.

The practice, though justified in different ways, was fundamentally a programme of cultural and racial assimilation with the aim of integrating those Aboriginal children deemed worthy or capable of salvation into mainstream society by removing them from the influence of their parents and other relatives. Australian governments were not alone in adopting a radical solution to problems posed by minority or opposition groups. During the same period the Canadian government forced Native Canadian children to attend residential schools, where they were supposed to unlearn their cultural ways and adopt the values of mainstream society. The Swiss government attempted to assimilate its Romany population by the same method. In the Middle Ages Christians engaged in the practice of abducting Jewish children, baptizing and raising them as Christians.[4] In the aftermath of the separation of East Timor from Indonesia, some members of the Indonesian militia rounded up and removed to West Papua large numbers of East Timorese children, with the apparent aim of indoctrinating them to support the integration of East Timor with Indonesia.

Most people have no hesitation in condemning such actions and policies as morally offensive – indeed, as serious injustices. The Canadian and Swiss governments have regarded it as appropriate to offer official apologies to Indian and Romany communities. Most Christians would agree with the teaching of St Jerome, which upholds the right of Jews to educate their children in their own faith.[5] But it is not easy to give an adequate account of the nature of the wrong: to explain why removing children is so unjust.

Condemnations of the policy of removing Aboriginal children usually concentrate on the harm done to the children themselves. Many of them fared badly. They were put into institutions where they were abused, mistreated, undernourished and denigrated. They were required to accept the values of whites in a society that refused to regard them as equals. They were often given only a minimal education and sent out to work for no pay. Children sent to foster families were also frequently abused and treated like slaves. But not all removed children suffered from deprivation or abuse. Some were treated well and were given opportunities they would never have had if they had stayed with their parents. Let us suppose that the policy had worked as its more well-meaning supporters thought it should work – that most children had been well treated, given a good education, had not suffered from discrimination, and had found a satisfactory position in mainstream society. However, these good consequences would not have made an unjust policy just. To take an analogous case, we would not think it justified to force poor people to give their children to rich families even if it could be proved that adoption would give these children far better chances in life.

In the case of the child removal policy practised in Australia, the parents and other members of Aboriginal families often suffered severely from the removal of their children. But the grief and despair they experienced do not provide either necessary or sufficient reasons for condemning abduction of children. Causing suffering to parents is not a necessary condition of injustice taking place. The parents of some of the Timorese children abducted by Indonesian militiamen were dead or missing, but this does not mean that it was right to take children away from their relatives and community. Nor is the pain suffered by parents and other relatives sufficient to explain why removing children is unjust. Many well-meaning people supposed that causing grief to Aboriginal parents was justified for the sake of the greater good of the children and society. We need to understand why this justification won't do.

The removal of Aboriginal children was an attempt to assimilate children to mainstream society – and perhaps ultimately to wipe out Aboriginal culture. Acts aimed at wiping out a culture or a religion are now widely condemned. But assimilation is not itself an evil. Cultures and religions do not have a right to exist independently of the desires and interests of their adherents or their impact on outsiders. Maintaining their culture or religion *is* often in the interests of members. Will Kymlicka identifies culture as a basic good – something individuals need in order to make meaningful choices and live worthwhile lives – and criticizes government policies that undermine minority cultures or fail to give them the support they need in order to survive.[6] However, his support for the right of individuals to a culture does not explain why child removal policies were so wrong. Abducted children successfully brought up in the mainstream culture acquired a cultural framework, and their adult relatives were not forced to abandon the one they had. In any case, not all acts of child removal can be construed as attempts to wipe out a culture or a religion. The stealing of Jewish children was too sporadic and unsystematic to count as an attempt to destroy Jewish culture or religion. It must be judged by its damage to relationships of other kinds.

The problem with all these attempts to understand the injustice of acts that remove children from their families in order to assimilate them, convert them or indoctrinate them is that they concentrate on harms done to the children or parents as individuals. So when these particular individuals are not harmed, or when their suffering seems to be justified by reference to a greater good for themselves or other individuals, it becomes difficult to explain what the injustice is. The injustice is better understood, I contend, as inflicting harm on the relationship between parents and children, or between kin and off-spring – and thus on individuals as members of family lines. They are wronged as children of particular parents or as parents of the re-moved children, and not merely as the particular individuals who they are. The wrong done to them can only be properly appreciated by reference to their relationship to members of their family. So understood, the child removal cases I have described are instances of what can be called 'injustices to family lines'.

Why was it wrong, in the cases discussed, to remove children from their parents and kin? There are several answers to this question. The first has already been explored. The family is the most important conduit for passing down from one generation to another things valued by individuals: their possessions, projects, responsibilities, values and traditions. Taking away children not only destroys the bond between children and parents, itself a cause of intense suffering; it also interferes in a drastic way with the lifetime-transcending inter-ests of parents and other kin. It breaks their connection with the future in a way that is likely to undermine their ability to live a meaningful life. But this is not the only reason for condemning child removal. People care about their offspring. They think it important to carry out their responsibilities to them, to give them a chance to acquire the values, traditions and heritage that they regard as valu-able. Removing children from their families is wrong, secondly, be-cause it prevents children from acquiring an inheritance – religious, political or cultural – that their parents value and think they ought to have. Of course, we can think of cases where it would be desirable to protect children from exposure to their parents' values. But unless we have a good reason to think that children will be seriously harmed by their relationship to their parents, we should accept and broaden the teaching of St Jerome and say that parents have an entitlement, so basic that it can be called 'natural', to bring up their children, or, in case of their deaths, have their children brought up, in their religion or culture or according to their fundamental beliefs. Any interference with this right, except for a very good reason, is not only an injustice to them, but also to their family lines. It harms the relationship that parents ought to be able to establish with their children.

A particularly important part of the heritage that people are entitled to pass on to their children is their culture and religion. Culture and in many cases religion are identity forming. By inheriting our culture, our descendants are able to regard our history, and the history of our community, as also belonging to them. It makes meaningful relationships between generations possible, and enables descendants to appreciate other things that we pass on to them. When this heritage is bound up with the learning of a language, it underwrites the very possibility of transgenerational communication. Children once grown are entitled to leave their culture or abandon their religion, but when they have grown up in the cultural or religious community of their parents, they are not so likely to lose the ability to maintain meaningful contact or the possibility of return. So a third reason for condemning child removal policies like those practised against Aboriginal families is that they destroy or undermine the possibility of meaningful relationships between members of families and their descendants.

A society ought to recognize the entitlement of parents to pass on their heritage, communal, cultural or merely familial, to their children – unless there is a very good reason for interference. And since the entitlement to pass on a culture or heritage is not simply something that parents care about during their lifetime, but is bound up with their lifetime-transcending interests, they are entitled to demand that their successors respect their wishes concerning their children in the event of their deaths. In most cases it is reasonable to suppose that they would have wished to have their children brought up by their relatives, or at least in their cultural or religious community.

Removal of children is not only a harm to parents. Family relationships locate individuals in a narrative, a history that explains to people where they come from and who they are, a story that connects their lives to the lives of their parents, ancestors and others from their culture or nation, and thus provides them with an identity that extends into the past before their birth. There is a widespread, perhaps a human, need for such an identity. Many of the Aborigines who were removed at birth from their parents and kin complain that they do not really know who they are. Most governments and adoption agencies now allow those who were adopted as children to trace and contact members of their biological family. But even if children do not suffer psychologically from lack of knowledge about their biological family, they have been wronged by being denied the inheritance and

heritage that they would have received from their family and community. Not receiving an entitlement is a wrong in respect to their status
as family members, whether or not this causes them suffering. The
nature of this wrong is something that would, presumably, be appreciated from what Rawls calls the perspective of representatives of
family lines – from the point of view of members of families who
are predisposed to insist that their descendants are entitled to receive
their cultural, religious and familial heritage.

A right to an inheritance, whether of property or culture, does not
last for ever. The mere fact that a person's mother or grandmother
was abducted from her family and raised by people of another culture
is no reason why she should complain of injustice, so long as she has a
secure place in the culture and society in which she was raised. In
many cases, however, circumstances ensure that the effects of such
injustices are transmitted from those wronged to their descendants. If
descendants of those who were removed from their family and culture
are never accepted or treated as equals in mainstream society – as so
often happened to Aborigines – then their lack of a connection to the
culture and community of their forebears makes them especially
vulnerable and insecure. They lack a proper place in the world. As
members of family lines, they too have been wronged by the injustice.
The representatives of family lines to whom Rawls gives the task of
determining principles of justice for their society will be predisposed
to demand of their successors that their children, grandchildren and
more remote descendants be protected from such wrongs.[7]

The existence of injustices to family lines is likely to have implications for the way we view reparative claims. If individuals can be
harmed as members of families, then we have an answer to a difficulty
outlined in chapter 7. It is a basic principle of reparative justice, as I
have pointed out, that individuals can demand reparation only for
injustices that harm them. The fact that they are members of a racial
or religious group against which injustices were directed does not give
them a reparative entitlement so long as harm done to these groups
has to be understood as harm done to particular individuals in them.
However, an injustice to family lines cannot be reduced to harms done
to particular individuals. Such injustices harm relationships between
parents and children, or forebears and descendants. Thus they harm
individuals as members of family lines, just as injustices to nations
harm individuals as citizens or members of nations. The existence of
such injustices opens the door to reparative claims for harms resulting
from a history of injustices to families. But to establish that members
of black families are entitled to reparation for a history of injustice
that includes slavery, we must first determine whether slavery and

other injustices committed against American blacks count as injustices to family lines.

Slavery as an injustice to family lines

An injustice against family lines is committed when the perpetrators seek to disrupt family relationships or wipe out family lines, keep members of family lines in perpetual slavery or submission, or attempt to prevent individuals from maintaining family relationships, carrying out family obligations, or receiving their inheritance as members of a family. To commit an injustice to family lines, perpetrators need not have as their main objective the persecution of families. Their attacks may be aimed at a religious, ethnic, political or racial group. Persecution counts as an injustice against family lines when it can only achieve its objective by undermining, disrupting, wiping out or subjugating families. Slavery as it was practised in the southern United States was clearly an injustice directed against family lines. Slave owners systematically thwarted attempts of slaves to maintain families or educate their children in their culture. Children were separated from their parents, husbands from wives; and every attempt was made to erase the cultural traditions which the slaves brought with them from Africa.

Furthermore, slavery as a system perpetuated itself, in part, by the enslavement of families. The children of slaves were also slaves. Once enslaved, a family was meant to remain in subjugation down through the generations. Slavery in the American South was different in this respect from the convict system that provided slave labour in Australia and colonial America. Convicts were freed once they had served their term. Children of convicts were free individuals from birth, and though they sometimes bore a stigma because of their parentage, their opportunities were not systematically thwarted, and some achieved high positions in their society. The convict system was unjust to many individuals, but it was no injustice to family lines.

Crimes committed with the intention of wiping out a religious or ethnic group – those labelled 'genocide' – are clearly injustices to family lines. The perpetrators do not single out particular individuals. They aim to destroy their opponents by wiping out families. But non-genocidal crimes – those that aim to destroy or undermine relationships in particular families – also count as injustices against family lines. Discrimination, as a systematic, long-term policy or practice, is such an injustice. The Jim Crow laws of the American South were measures intended to keep black families in a subordinate position –

to perpetuate their subjugation down through the generations. Not only were African Americans denied rights and opportunities enjoyed by whites. Segregated schools and a segregated labour force ensured that black children would be relegated generation after generation to menial occupations that serviced the white community. Discrimination in the North was not generally maintained by law, but it was so widespread and systematic that it is reasonable to believe that it had the same purpose: to perpetuate subordination of black people – to prevent their children from ever obtaining (except in very small numbers) the opportunities available to whites. Immigrants from Europe were also subject to discrimination, and often forced to accept poorly paid jobs, but their children were not prevented from obtaining the advantages and opportunities that had been denied to their parents. Discrimination against immigrants, the occasional or local discrimination that has been visited on members of particular religious and ethnic groups, is injustice to individuals, not injustice against family lines.

Social and economic disadvantages tend to run in families. Children of working-class parents are less likely than middle-class children to do well at school, get a higher education, or obtain a well-paying job. Do class disadvantages perpetuated in families constitute an injustice against family lines? In some cases they can be so described. Education in early industrial Britain and similar countries was largely a privilege of the well-to-do, and working-class families had virtually no opportunities to improve their position in society. The government and privileged classes may not have had a deliberate policy of perpetuating the disadvantages suffered by working-class families, but their failure to do anything about the conditions that condemned these families, generation after generation, to deprivation counts as an injustice to family lines. On the other hand, in countries where education is universal, and there is no discrimination against people with a working-class background (and where, in fact, many working-class children improve their social position), it is less plausible to say this. An injustice that wrongs individuals may have bad effects on their children, yet not count as an injustice against family lines so long as the children are not prevented from making use of the opportunities offered by their society or from obtaining the resources to which justice as equity entitles them.

These remarks, though brief, should be enough to establish that injustices against family lines are wrongs of a distinct kind. When Robinson insists that black Americans continue to suffer from the legacy of slavery, he can be interpreted as claiming that they suffer harm as members of family lines. According to his argument, they have been deprived by slavery and other injustices of their African heritage, and denied a positive, affirmative place in American history. These are deprivations individuals can suffer only because they are related to the past through their family lines. Let us assume that Robinson is right about the nature of the harm, and right to suppose that it has resulted in psychological damage to black Americans which has also had an effect on their material well-being. The question remains whether it is reasonable to attribute to slavery the harm which black Americans suffer as members of family lines.

One of the arguments against black reparations for slavery can be quickly dismissed. The fact that presently existing African Americans would not have been born if their ancestors had not been enslaved is no barrier to their claiming reparation for slavery as members of family lines. For their claim rests not on their being the particular individuals they are, but on their membership of a family line to which an injustice was done. In this respect, their position is no different from that of people who claim reparation as members of a nation, and no more problematic. However, to justify reparations to black Americans for slavery, we must also answer Bittker's objection to the idea that individuals can be owed reparation for an injustice that happened long before their birth.

Between the time when slavery ended and the present, American governments have committed or failed to prevent further injustices to black families. If these injustices had not been done, if former slaves or their descendants had been given a chance to improve their position and to construct for themselves and their families a positive identity as free and equal Americans, the harms that Robinson describes would probably not exist. Unfortunately this did not happen. Bittker's point is that the very fact that governments could have acted differently, and would have done so if they had been just, indicates that the blame for present harms should fall not on slavery, but on these other, more recent injustices. This argument is plausible so long as we concentrate on individuals themselves and ignore their relation to others. It is reasonable to insist that the harms suffered by individuals to their well-being or prospects should be attributed only to wrongs done to *them*, or at most to wrongs done to their immediate forebears that have an 'automatic effect' on their well-being. The fact that these wrongs have a causal history that can be traced back to slavery seems irrelevant to their case for reparation. When individuals are harmed as members of family lines, however, Bittker's argument is not so compelling. For family lines are transgenerational relationships with a long history, and understanding the nature of these injustices may require us to acknowledge a connection between recent and more ancient wrongs.

From the perspective of members of family lines, the history outlined by Bittker tells a different story. The injustices that occurred after the Civil War and up to recent times were not independent wrongs. They were part of an intrinsically connected history of injustices. This history includes the failures of governments to alleviate the harm caused to black families by slavery and, worse, attempts, allowed or even supported by governments, to maintain black dependence and subordination by different means. It is this history of injustice, which includes slavery, to which the harms described by Robinson should be attributed. In other words, injuries to memory and self-esteem, and at least some part of the consequences of these injuries, can be blamed on a history of injustices which destroyed the heritage of African American families and denied them an opportunity to regain it or to establish a sound basis for an identity as Americans. It is for the harms caused by this history that presently existing black Americans deserve reparation. Slavery is relevant to their case for reparation.

The argument I have offered in defence of black reparations is similar to my defence in chapter 4 of Sioux demands for reparation. Just as the Sioux can demand reparation for a history of injustice that includes dispossession that took place many generations ago, so too can members of black families demand reparation for a history of injustice that includes slavery. The Sioux are making a claim as members of a nation to which injustices have been done; black Americans as members of family lines which have suffered injustices. The Sioux, I argued, are justified in demanding reparation that alleviates or compensates them for harms that can be blamed on the history of injustices to their nation. What reparation can black Americans legitimately demand?

Reparation for a history of injustice

Reparation should remove, or at least alleviate, the harm done, and in doing so bring about reconciliation between descendants of victims and members of the nation or organizations that committed the injustices. Reconciliation in the cases I have been considering would involve demonstrating respect for those wronged, acknowledging that wrongs occurred, undoing harm, and taking measures to assure members of wronged families that they and their family lines will be respected in the future. The measures proposed by the Australian Human Rights and Equal Opportunity Commission were designed to bring about this result in the case of removed Aboriginal children.

Its report recommended, among other things, that an official apology be made to those who were removed from their families and to the families and communities from which they were taken, that future injustices of this kind be prevented through programmes of education, that those harmed be compensated, and that services for finding relatives and making contacts with kin be made available to them.[8] Robinson thinks that the harm done to American blacks by slavery and other injustices would be alleviated by 'owning up to slavery', and by programmes to rebuild self-esteem of blacks by connecting them to their African heritage and by making the contributions of black Americans visible in the symbols, legends and monuments of the nation.[9] What he is suggesting are measures that would reconcile members of black American families to their nation – make them able to think of themselves and past and future members of their families as respected participants in American society.

However, most advocates of black reparations think that much more is required. James Forman demanded $500 million from churches and synagogues, which he regarded as 'only a beginning of the reparations due us as people who have been exploited and degraded, brutalized, killed and persecuted'.[10] Boxill insists that white Americans should return the benefits they have received from the stolen labour of slaves. Robinson says that blacks are owed 'massive restitutions'. Attempts have been made to determine the amount of reparation using estimates of the income that slaves should have earned and the compounded interest that would have accrued to these earnings.[11]

These demands for reparation face conceptual as well as political difficulties. Claims appealing to unjust enrichment of whites at the expense of blacks, if taken literally, depend on the idea that descendants of victims of injustice are heirs to property that was wrongly taken from their ancestors. We have seen that rights of property and inheritance can be defended within limits. But it is doubtful, for reasons already discussed, that this justification can succeed when the wrong occurred so long ago, especially when there is no way of tracing who took what from whom, and no way of determining (and perhaps no way of making a meaningful inquiry into) what heirs would have received if the injustices had not been done. It is safe to say that individuals in black families would have been, on average, better off relative to individuals in white families if the injustices had not occurred, or if reparation had been made at an earlier time. But an appeal to the duty to make reparation cannot justify a general transfer of wealth from whites to blacks. To count as appropriate compensation, payments surely ought to be made to individuals or families

according to the wrong they have suffered. They are not owed reparation simply because they are black or suffer greater disadvantages
than other Americans.

Those who appeal to unjust enrichment probably do not mean to
be taken so literally. They are not defending the inheritance claims of
members of particular family lines. They are pointing out that blacks
are among the most disadvantaged groups in the United States
according to all social indicators, and they plausibly trace the cause
of these disadvantages to a history of systematic discrimination and
mistreatment from which most whites have benefited in one way or
another. The demand of black Americans for reparation is really a
demand for a redistribution of resources to close the gap between the
living standards of white and black Americans, or for measures that
increase opportunities available to African Americans.[12]

However, this understanding of what it means to undo the effects of
unjust enrichment seems to confuse the demands of justice as equity
with reparative justice. Compensating for unjust disadvantages and
making society more equal are important objectives according to
many theories of justice as equity (for example, that of Rawls). But
they are different objectives from those of reparative justice. If supporters of black reparations are really demanding equity, then the fact
that wrongs were done to black families in the past seems irrelevant.
If what they are demanding is reparation, they are faced with the
problem of justifying programmes that give benefits to people just
because they happen to be disadvantaged members of a particular
racial group. This objection leads to another. If equity is the real
objective, then how can we justify a policy or a demand that singles
out for special attention, or provides special advantages to, just one
group of disadvantaged people. Some communities or categories of
white Americans (not to mention people in other groups) also suffer
economic disadvantages. A programme which gives priority to removing the disadvantages of black Americans thus seems to violate
ideas of equity that are central to its justification – particularly if
equally disadvantaged people in other groups have to make sacrifices
for the sake of removing black disadvantage.

This latter difficulty inevitably arises in debates about reverse discrimination policies. These programmes focus on particular groups
which have suffered from a history of injustice, and provide their
members with special benefits or opportunities that people from other
groups cannot claim. Reverse discrimination is justified sometimes as
compensating for past injustices, and sometimes as a means for
making society more equitable in the future. But whatever justification is used, one objection that is bound to arise is that such pro-

grammes unfairly benefit people just because they happen to be members of a particular disadvantaged group, and provide no benefits for and may even require sacrifices from, equally disadvantaged individuals who are not group members.[13]

Those who make these objections are in one important respect right. As far as access to resources is concerned, black Americans are owed no more but no less than what is required to remove the unjust disadvantages that they and their families presently suffer. They are owed no more than they can claim on grounds of equity – no more than what is owed to others who suffer from similar disadvantages. But it does not follow that the American nation would have no remaining reparative responsibilities to blacks once it properly acknowledged past injustices. Reparative justice may require that black families be given special consideration in ways that do not offend against principles of equity.

Equity and special consideration

Let us suppose that everyone in American society is in agreement about what justice as equity requires, and suppose too that Americans are determined to achieve equity for all. If this objective could be achieved for everyone at once, then black Americans would have no basis for complaining about injustice – so long as historical wrongs done to their families were also properly acknowledged. They, along with everyone else, would have received all they can reasonably demand. But it is unrealistic to suppose that justice can be accomplished so quickly and so completely even in a society of people dedicated to the ideal of equity. Where injustice is multifaceted and deeply embedded in the social fabric, a transition to a just society is likely to be costly and disruptive. Different measures may be required for different cases, and trying to implement all of them at one time may have unforeseen and counter-productive effects. In these circumstances, a society is justified in transforming itself in stages: concentrating first on removing some forms of injustice, or injustice to some groups of people, and later removing injustices that take other forms. Under these conditions or, for that matter, in a society where people are not so single-mindedly committed to achieving equity, it would be just to give priority to those families who have suffered from a history of wrongs. In particular, reparative considerations give us grounds for giving priority to black Americans over people whose disadvantages do not stem from injustices to family lines (or whose families were done injustices of a lesser kind).

The priority extended to members of black families can be justified by a number of closely related considerations. Injustices to family lines are serious wrongs; they are injustices from which Rawls's representatives of family lines will be particularly concerned to protect their descendants. These representatives can be expected to demand that their successors give priority to alleviating harm done to their descendants by these injustices. Since this perspective, and the priorities to which it gives rise, are justified by the importance of families to individuals and social life, we have good reason for endorsing their demand.

Furthermore, harms caused by injustices to family lines are likely to be more serious than harms caused by wrongs to individuals. American blacks do not suffer merely from economic disadvantages relative to whites, but also from a loss of heritage and the lack of a source of positive identification. As a result, they are more likely to regard themselves as marginal, disregarded members of American society. Because of a history of injustices (Robinson claims), blacks are more likely to be alienated from the political process, sceptical about their role in American life, and despairing about the future of themselves and their children. Giving priority to removing black disadvantage would help to undo these harms by demonstrating a national determination to overcome the past and include African Americans as equal citizens – which is what reparation as reconciliation requires.

The nature of the wrongs done to black families is likely to justify giving them priority over other groups whose members have suffered injustices to family lines. Imagine an isolated poor white community whose needs have been ignored for generations. Because of their lack of educational opportunities, children have little chance of escaping into mainstream society, and as a result are doomed to live in the same poverty as their parents. Neglect in this case is an injustice not only to particular individuals, but also to members of family lines. Though the suffering of these families demands a remedy, the harm that members suffer as a consequence of a history of neglect is likely to be less serious than the harm suffered by members of black families as the result of a history of slavery and deliberate discrimination. Members of the white community have not been deprived of their heritage; their identity as a community is likely to be secure, and indeed, they may retain a positive, proud view of their history and place in American society.

By taking into account the existence and degree of harm to individuals as members of family lines, and what is required to bring about reconciliation between those wronged and their nation, we can justify singling out people of a certain kind and giving them priority as our first step in making society more equitable for everyone. In particular, we can justify programmes that give priority to members of disadvantaged African-American families. One of the objections to reverse discrimination has been answered. This does not mean that giving black Americans special advantages in competitions for jobs or university places is the best way of alleviating harms done to black families. Other objections to reverse discrimination, as it has been practised, need to be answered. Programmes of other kinds may be better means of overcoming disadvantages – particularly of those black families whose members are not in a position to take advantage of reverse discrimination policies. The question of what exactly should be done to repair harm done to family lines is not answered by this investigation. What it has established is that there is no incompatibility between the requirements of equity and the demands of reparative justice. In the framework of a reconciliatory approach to reparation, they remain distinct, but do not come into conflict.

The theory in perspective

How can individuals who are not themselves the victims of an injustice but merely descendants of the victims claim reparation? In this part of my study I have reinterpreted and defended two common answers to this question. I have argued, first of all, that descendants of victims can have rights of inheritance to possessions unjustly taken from their forebears. Their right to receive an inheritance does not follow from a theory of historical title that includes an unquestionable right of bequest. It is underwritten by lifetime-transcending interests of individuals, the importance to individuals of family and friendships, and, most of all, by the role that families play in the lives of individuals and within nations. Being a descendant of victims of injustice is sufficient in many cases to justify a reparative entitlement to an inheritance. The burden of proof is more likely to fall on those who deny the claim. I have argued, secondly, that individuals as members of families may be entitled to claim reparation for harms that result from wrongs done to their family lines. Though families are not themselves agents, their members can be owed reparation for harm done by a history of injustices which may include relatively ancient injustices like slavery as well as more recent wrongs.

This second conclusion is likely to create disquiet. How far do the reparative responsibilities of nations extend? If African Americans can claim reparation for a history of injustice that includes slavery, does that mean that Africans themselves can claim reparation from those nations that encouraged or benefited from the slave trade? Do nations bear a reparative responsibility for all the damages to family lines that they may have caused sometime in their past history? To answer these questions, or indicate how they should be answered, we have to chart the limitations that can reasonably be imposed on reparative claims.

Descendants of victims are owed reparation for an injustice if and only if two conditions are satisfied. First, they must either be the designated or presumed heirs to the property of a victim of unjust dispossession (where other requirements of justice are satisfied), or members of a family line who continue to suffer from a harm that can be attributed to the injustice or to an interrelated history of injustice that includes the injustice in question. Second, the injustice must have been committed by an existing nation (or a nation whose responsibilities have been taken over by an existing nation) or some other presently existing, organized, transgenerational association. The second condition rules out reparation for harms for which no existing agent can be made responsible. Individuals, cultures, ethnic or racial groups cannot be held responsible for reparation for historical injustices. Nor can Western civilization, or even Western imperialism.

The first condition rules out demands for reparation for injustices to which present harms cannot be attributed. Suppose that several centuries ago traders, looking for a profitable line of business, encouraged leaders of small but prosperous African nations to sell them the prisoners of war whom they held in captivity. So profitable and widespread did this trade become that soon African nations were making war on each other in order to capture prisoners. These wars, and other politically destabilizing effects of the slave trade, devastated the region, and made it easy prey in later times to imperialists and colonists. As a result of its history, the population of the region is now living in poverty.

This story is not meant to be an accurate account of the relations between Westerners and the people of eastern and central Africa. This would require much more detail. What it illustrates is a point made by Sher about attribution of harm. African history seems different in important respects from the history of Africans in America. The injustices done by governments to American blacks after the Civil War are best understood, I have argued, as failures to undo harms caused by slavery, or as attempts to perpetuate the subordination of black families by different means – in other words, as injustices whose nature can be understood only in relation to slavery. This is what allows us to attribute present harms to a history that includes slavery. African history is much more complex, and probably cannot be regarded as following a single agenda. The slave trade may have been the cause that initiated the downward spiral of African fortunes. But it is probably not the wrong to which present harms can be attributed. This harm is the result of many different factors: war, imperialism, colonialism and, more recently, the effects of world trade and global politics. Many agents with different objectives, sometimes acting at cross-purposes, have produced the unhappy results.

In so far as this is true, present harms suffered by Africans cannot be attributed to the slave trade, and members of African family lines cannot demand reparations from any nation for this injustice. It does not follow that they cannot demand reparations for other injustices done by Western nations. More recent actions of colonists and imperialists, in so far as they perpetuated subordination and dependence, also count as injustices against family lines. It seems plausible to suppose that some of the harms and disadvantages now suffered by Africans can be attributed to a history that includes these wrongs. But even if this were not so – even if present harms were the unfortunate and unintended result of actions of many different agents for which no existing nation, company or religious group could be blamed – it does not follow that wealthy individuals and nations have no responsibility for undoing the effects. Most theories of justice as equity say that those who benefit from interactions ought to share with those who suffer loss. Making commitments or doing wrongs are not the only ways in which agents accrue responsibility for the past. A theory of reparation is only one part of an account of what we owe to those with whom we share a history and a world.

Conclusion: Justice and Transgenerational Relationships

A political society, according to Edmund Burke 'is a partnership between those who are living, those who are dead, and those yet to be born'.[1] He puts forward this idea of political relationships in opposition to contractual theories of political association, which ignore history and tradition, and derive rights and responsibilities of citizens from the agreements that rational individuals would be prepared to make with each other. Burke believed that we have obligations with respect to our political predecessors, and ought to keep faith with the political traditions and institutions we have inherited from the past. The position I have been defending is not the political conservatism associated with Burke. It does not require us to conserve or even respect our political institutions. It is not a bulwark against radical reform or revolution. However, it has in common with Burke's position the idea that some of our obligations as members of nations derive from a transgenerational partnership.

We impose responsibilities on our successors, and in turn acquire responsibilities with respect to the deeds and interests of our predecessors. The collective responsibility of members of nations encompasses the deeds of their predecessors. My view, like that of Burke, insists on the moral importance of transgenerational relationships between members of nations and members of families. It takes seriously the fact that a nation is an intergenerational association, and it is implicitly critical of those views about justice, responsibility and rights that ignore the historical dimension of our social existence.

Many theories of justice and right in the Western tradition are what might be described as 'synchronic'. They concentrate on relations between contemporaries. They derive their ideas about just relations from a consideration of the ways in which interactions benefit or harm individuals, or by imagining what individuals would consent to as a basis for co-operative relations. Those who put forward synchronic theories tend to regard entitlements as claims that individuals can make on others, and assign obligations only to those who incurred their responsibilities through their consent, their actions or their role in collective action. But living people played no role in the deeds of their predecessors. And the victims of historical injustices are mostly dead. They can make no claims on the living for what they suffered, and their lives cannot be made better or worse by anything we do. We are not in relationships of co-operation with people of the past, and we cannot reach an agreement with them. A synchronic theory would find it difficult, if not impossible, to countenance responsibilities with respect to past people or entitlements that arise from historical injustices, and few theorists have turned their attention to the problem. From a synchronic point of the view, Burke's idea of a partnership with past generations makes no sense.

However, historical obligations and entitlements do exist, and are of considerable moral importance. This study defends the idea that reparative justice must encompass obligations and entitlements that are historical, and at the same time it makes a case against synchronic approaches to justice. It provides a reason for rejecting theories of justice that ignore, deny or downplay responsibilities that are so central to just relations in political societies and international society. It is a contribution to an approach to justice which focuses on transgenerational entitlements and obligations – a theory that could be described as 'diachronic'. What such a theory would be like, and how exactly it would challenge existing views of justice, is beyond the scope of this study. However, in this concluding chapter I will outline some of the topics that such a theory would probably need to encompass.

Future generations and sustainability

Most of us would agree that 'no generation is at liberty to ransack the environment, or to overload the earth with more people than can be supported'.[2] Environmental concerns have forced public officials to incorporate the objective of 'sustainability' into their planning policies, and philosophers to include duties to future generations in their theories of justice. However, duties to future people, to individuals who do not now exist, put a severe strain on synchronic theories. We cannot bargain or discourse with future people, make agreements with them, or determine exactly what their interests will be. Worse, we do not even know how many of them there will be. Their very existence depends on what we do. So if entitlements belong only to those who can claim them, if doing right or wrong is a matter of benefiting or harming identifiable individuals, if justice presupposes co-operative relationships, or if we cannot be in relationships of justice with beings who have no way of affecting us for better or worse (as synchronic theories have often implied), then it is difficult to make sense of the belief that we have duties to future people.[3] On the other hand, if we avoid such problems by adopting a holist objective – if, for example, we aim to promote the greatest overall good of humankind – we could be faced with distasteful consequences. Promoting this general good may require us to increase the number of future humans even to the point where the well-being of each future human decreases – so long as we are increasing the *total amount* of good.[4]

Because synchronic approaches are not in a good position to deal with duties to future generations, those who regard it as imperative to include them have been forced to introduce additional assumptions into their theories. Laslett speaks of a 'tri-generational contract' between present, past and future generations – though the fact that past and future generations cannot participate in decision making puts a severe strain on the contract metaphor.[5] Rawls introduces a diachronic dimension into his theory by supposing that those who determine principles of justice for their society are not merely individuals but 'heads of families' – people who represent family lines and presumably care enough about the well-being of their children and grandchildren to want to insure that their interests will be protected.

What makes Rawls's theory diachronic is not merely the interest of representatives of family lines in the well-being of their descendants, but the fact that their relation to future people is essential to their reasoning about what existing members of a society owe to their successors. We are supposed to determine what we ought to save for our descendants by considering what we think we are entitled to claim from our forebears.[6] By insisting that duties arise from a relationship between generations, his approach avoids the problem of not being able to identify future people. Representatives of family lines are concerned about the well-being of their descendants and successors, whoever they turn out to be. I made use of this idea in my discussion of right of inheritance and reparation for injustices to family lines in chapters 8 and 9.

Whether Rawls's approach is an adequate solution to problems concerning future generations is not clear. Environmentalists point out that some of the harms that we can do to future people (for example, by the deposit of nuclear wastes) require that our moral concern stretch further than a few generations. But there is another problem that he shares with most of those who have put forward views about duties to future generations. The diachronic approach to the problem of future generations bears an uncertain relation to his theory as a whole. Though he suggests that the individuals who make a decision in the 'original position' about principles of justice can be thought of as representatives of families, he has almost nothing to say about how this perspective might bear on other issues of justice. So it is easy to ignore the diachronic dimension of his theory, as most of his critics have done, and to assume that those who make an agreement are simply 'disinterested' individuals in a society of contemporaries.[7]

Preservation of heritage and duties to the dead

Burke believed that we should participate in the partnership between the living, the dead and the not yet born by maintaining the political institutions and social traditions that we have inherited from our ancestors and passing them on to our descendants. Though many people reject Burke's political conservatism, most of us are conservatives about some aspects of our heritage. We think we ought to preserve and pass on to future generations the monuments and buildings associated with our history, or that we should maintain the character of our neighbourhoods, the natural environments that we have become attached to, or some of the rituals of our society that connect us to past generations. However, it is not so easy to justify preserving a heritage, particularly when doing so requires sacrifices. Not everything that people want to preserve is aesthetically outstanding; not everyone thinks that it is important to maintain a connection with the past or to respect what past people created.

The issues raised in debates about preservation of heritage are similar to those raised by question of whether we have duties to or in respect to the dead (which I discussed briefly in chapter 8). Like the people of future generations, past people do not exist. We cannot make agreements with them; we are not in relationships of co-operation with them. Moreover, we seem to have no reason to make them the objects of our concern. We can harm future people by what we do, but the dead, most people suppose, are beyond being harmed by us, and this makes it difficult to understand how we have duties to them or why we should do anything for their sake. Most philosophers seem to assume that the dead can be safely ignored. But the fact remains that most of us think that we do have duties in respect to past people.

If we do have duties to, or in respect to, the dead, then we still have to decide what these duties are and how seriously we should treat them. Some people think that we owe it to the people of the past to honour them for their sacrifices, or to respect what they accomplished.[8] Others have no such conception of their duties. The issue is not merely whose side we should take, but how we should decide the matter. I suggested that our obligations with respect to the dead are best understood from a diachronic perspective by determining what demands living people are entitled to make of their survivors. But a theory able to explain what duties we have with respect to the deeds, creations, desires and interests of people of the past has not yet been developed. Not much progress will be made so long as the synchronic orientation of existing theories makes it difficult to countenance such duties, let alone explain what they are.

The value of intergenerational institutions

A diachronic theory need not support Burke's philosophy, but it is likely to have something to say about the moral value of institutions and political practices that enable members of nations to hand on responsibilities to their successors and underwrite legitimate requests that people direct to their survivors. It should be able to explain what is valuable about intergenerational societies.

Synchronic theories do not do this. They recognize that many human associations, above all nations, are intergenerational, and that their members generally want to perpetuate their institutions, and the political values they protect, down through the generations. But they have little to say about the importance of transgenerational relationships and the value to members of political societies of the institutions that underwrite these relationships. This lack is associated with a chronic problem in political philosophy – that of explaining why members of a political society should accept and be bound by the commitments entered into by their predecessors.

In classical political philosophy this problem has often surfaced as the problem of explaining why we have an obligation to comply with the laws and political institutions of our nation. If members of a political society have freely consented to be governed by the laws and institutions of their state (as in the fiction of the social contract), then the reason for its authority and their obedience is clear. The problem arises because most of us have never made this commitment. The responsibilities of citizenship are imposed on us without our ever having a chance to consent to them (or refuse our consent). However, the problem of political obligation can be understood as a particular instance of a more general difficulty that arises whenever people are expected to accept an obligation to which they did not consent (either as individuals or through their role in a collective decision-making process) or one that they did not incur through their own actions. One of the main issues I have discussed in this study – how people can be required to take responsibility for the commitments and deeds of their predecessors or the consequences of these deeds – is another instance of this general problem. Because they take as their paradigm relationships between individuals who acquire responsibilities through their interactions with others, synchronic theories have a difficult time accepting or accounting for any of these 'non-voluntary' obligations.

I have argued that we do, nevertheless, have some obligations of this kind. As members of nations we are responsible for keeping the commitments made by our predecessors (all things being equal); we have an obligation to make reparation for their injustices to other nations and to family lines. We are obliged to fulfil their just demands. These obligations exist because our lifetime-transcending concerns as citizens, members of families or individuals give us moral reasons for maintaining a practice of keeping the commitments of our predecessors and repairing the wrongs they have done, and fulfilling some of the requests of those now dead. A diachronic political theory would have to consider the ways in which these practices are supported and underwritten by political and social institutions, and what that tells us about the value of these institutions and the political societies to which they belong.

The diachronic approach is predicated on basic facts about human existence: that people not yet born can be benefited or harmed by what we do; that the fulfilment of requests and demands made by those now dead depend on the actions of their survivors; that historical wrongs can blight the lives of existing people. It draws attention to the importance of transgenerational relationships and the obligations and entitlements associated with them. This study has investigated some of these obligations and entitlements. It thus contributes to an appreciation of the partnership between generations as a moral relationship that requires us to take responsibility for our nation's past as well as making provisions for its future.

Notes

Introduction: History and Responsibility

1 For a summary and discussion of the 'Black Manifesto' see Bedau, 1972.
2 Browne, 1991. See also Magee, 1993.
3 See also Rao, 1981.
4 Barkan discusses Clinton's apology to native Hawaiians (2000, pp. 216ff) and Queen Elizabeth's apology to the Maoris (p. 264). The South African Truth and Reconciliation Commission is described in Minow, 1998, ch. 4. Japan's apology is reported by Desmond (1995); the Pope's statement by Stanley (2000); and the apology of the Canadian government by Bourrie (1998).
5 John Howard, speech to the Australian Reconciliation Convention in Melbourne, Australia, 26 May 1997. Apologies were nevertheless presented by some Australian churches and state governments and by numerous individuals. Brooks presents the debate in the USA about apology for slavery (1999b, pp. 352–4).
6 Barkan, 2000, p. xvi.
7 Nozick, 1974, pp. 150–3.
8 Boxill, 1972, pp. 119–20.
9 Even if we take Nozick's 'formula' seriously, there are enormous difficulties in applying it. Some of the problems associated with transgenerational restitution are discussed by Cowan (1997) and Litan (1977).
10 See Barkan's account of Jewish responses to Germany's offer of reparations for Nazi atrocities (2000, pp. 23–7).
11 Boxill, 1972, p. 118.
12 These reasons for restitution are put forward by Barkan (2000, pp. xv–xxiv).

13　Kymlicka, 1995, p. 116. Kymlicka allows, however, that appeals to history have some moral force.

14　Lyons, 1977, p. 268. His views will be discussed in more detail in ch. 4.

15　Robert Penn Warren, quoted in Bittker, 1973, pp. 9–10.

16　Bittker, 1973, p. 12.

17　Robinson, 2000, p. 216.

18　Brooks, 1999a, p. 7.

Chapter 1　Treaties and Transgenerational Responsibilities

1　Orange (1987) provides a history of the treaty and its aftermath. Sharp (1999) discusses the development of Maori movements since the 1980s.

2　French, 1994, pp. 38–41.

3　I assume here that nations can inherit responsibilities from other nations. I will defend this assumption in ch. 5.

4　'Vienna Convention on the Law of Treaties', in Brownlie, 1995.

5　McNair, 1961, pp. 493.

6　My way of using the term 'nation', though based on precedent, may cause difficulties. In discussions of nationalism, the term is usually used to mean a group of people who share the same culture, religion, history or historical legends. Such groups may not be self-governing. A nation, according to my definition, is essentially a *political* entity whose members may share a culture, but may not. If my use of the term causes confusion, this is regrettable, but there seems to be no better alternative. The term 'state' is too much associated with a particular kind of political society; 'community' is too vague (and suggests a 'togetherness' that not all nations possess); and 'peoples' is no less problematic than 'nations'.

7　I am relying on an intuitive understanding of what promising means, and not on any particular philosopher's account. I believe that what I say about promises could as easily be endorsed by a rule utilitarian as by a deontologist.

8　The conflict between democratic principles and treaty obligations is played out in US courts. 'As a matter of domestic law within the United States, Congress may override a pre-existing treaty.... To do so, however, would place the United States in breach of the obligation owed under international law to its treaty partner(s) to honor the treaty or agreement in good faith. Consequently, courts in the United States are disinclined to find that Congress has actually intended to override a treaty or other internationally binding obligation. Instead, they struggle to interpret the Congressional act and/or the international instrument in such a way as to reconcile the two' (Kirgis, 1997).

9　Why should citizens of a democracy who opposed an agreement or didn't vote for the leader who made it nevertheless be required to fulfil it? This is a question about why and to what extent we are required to accept the practices that make it possible for a democracy to function.

This is an important issue, but different from the one I am discussing. I simply assume that in many cases we should accept the obligations incurred by our democratically elected leaders.

10 Nozick (1974) does not discuss treaties, but there is nothing in his position that would prevent him from acknowledging that treaties and promises give rise to special obligations. I am presenting an argument that might be made by someone who adopts his views.

11 I will discuss arguments concerning historical titles in ch. 4.

12 Feinberg, 1968, p. 687. He briefly discusses, but seems to dismiss, a way in which individuals might have responsibility without control (pp. 687–8).

13 Bigelow, Pargetter and Young, 1990, p. 335.

14 Most discussions, it seems to me, run together the two interpretations. Bigelow, Pargetter and Young (1990) do so. They think that a causal link between the actions of one group of people and unjustified harm suffered by another is enough to establish a 'weak' case for compensation. The existence of systematic injustice only makes the case stronger. My contention is that the weak case for compensation is really a case for justice as equity, but the issue of what distinguishes justice as equity from reparative justice needs further discussion (which I provide in ch. 3).

15 See Goff and Jones, 1993. A basic principle of the law of restitution is that a person should not benefit from his or her criminal or unjust actions (p. 703). But this principle does not deny to descendants the benefits they have reaped from the wrongdoing of their forebears. The law allows that people may be liable to pay for benefits that they didn't ask to receive, but liability does not exist for benefits accrued generations after the debt was incurred (pp. 22ff).

16 This point is elaborated by Waldron (1992, p. 18). The issues will be discussed in more detail in ch. 6.

17 MacIntyre, 1981, p. 220.

18 Scheffler (1997) defends non-voluntary special responsibilities, but does not specify what associations give us these responsibilities.

19 Gilbert, 1996.

20 Simmons makes a similar point (1996, p. 258).

21 Jedlicki, 1990, p. 55.

22 Article 26 of the Vienna Convention on the Law of Treaties (Brownlie, 1995, p. 391).

23 Hare (1963, ch. 6), insists that acceptance of this rule is a necessary condition for making moral judgements. I do not hold so strong a thesis. There may be areas of personal morality where the rule does not apply. However, it is difficult to imagine that there would be any cases of moral reasoning about public issues that do not presuppose it.

24 See Articles 49 and 51 of the Vienna Convention on the Law of Treaties (Brownlie, 1995, p. 40).

25 Some of the contemporary debate is about the meaning and significance of the Maori term 'rangatiratanga' that was included in the version of

the treaty signed by Maori chiefs. This word is untranslatable, but means something like 'sovereign authority'. The suggestion is that Maoris who signed the treaty believed that they were retaining their independent authority. No such implication is contained in the English version. For a discussion of some of the difficulties associated with the interpretation of treaties, see Goodin, 2000, pp. 324ff.

Chapter 2   Historical Injustice and Respect for Nations

1   Wheeler (1997) defends a view of reparation that depends on believing that our ancestors were decent people, that they would have recognized their actions to be wrong and wanted to do something to right these wrongs if they had only been free of the prejudices of their times. His view has the serious drawback that we have no reason to make reparation for the deeds of ancestors who were not decent people – as he admits.
2   Costo and Henry, 1977, p. 6.
3   Natural law theories gave way in the nineteenth century to legal positivism, a doctrine that denies that law requires a moral basis. Moreover, it became increasingly common to deny that indigenous nations had rights of sovereignty. Size, power and having a European style of government came to be criteria for being worthy of consideration in international society. I will take it without further argument that these criteria are irrelevant from a moral point of view. For an account of changing attitudes to indigenous nations, see Anaya, 1996.
4   Walzer, 1977, p. 54.
5   Laslett assumes that transgenerational obligations are owed only in respect to deeds of *ancestors*, and thus dismisses the idea that Americans (whose ancestors came from many different places) could owe reparations for slavery (1992, pp. 39–43). I reject the assumption. The fact that the ancestors of many Americans had nothing to do with slavery does not stand in the way of the claim that Americans owe reparation for slavery. Whether they do is something I discuss in Part II.
6   A person can, to be sure, make a provision in his will that the resources of his estate be used to pay a debt or keep a promise, and we generally suppose that a society ought to ensure that such provisions are honoured. Ensuring that the terms of a will are fulfilled is a societal, not a family, responsibility. I will consider what reasons can be given for the existence of this responsibility in ch. 8.

Chapter 3   Theories of Reparation

1   Lamont, 1941, p. 18. Lamont, like many writers on legal philosophy, uses the term 'distributive' rather than 'positive' justice. I have chosen the latter term because in political philosophy 'distributive justice' is often

used to refer to egalitarian or meritocratic theories that demand the redistribution of resources among members of a society according to need, desert or some other principle – fulfilling what I call requirements of equity. Positive theories of justice encompass Nozick's theory of right, as well as egalitarian or meritocratic principles of justice.

2   For example, Rawls in *A Theory of Justice* takes as his primary concern what he calls 'strict compliance theory' – that is, an ideal theory that assumes perfect compliance with principles of justice. The problems of justice in a society in which compliance is only partial, he thinks, can only be understood in the light of such a theory (1971, pp. 8–9).

3   Another possible reason is that crime in Western legal systems is regarded as an offence against the state, not against the individuals who are the victims. In the past there have been no mechanisms for forcing criminals to make reparation to their victims, and thus not much reason for legal theorists to think about the issues raised by reparation.

4   These assumptions are found in Nozick, 1974, pp. 150–3. He regards the interpretation and application of the second principle to be problematic, but does not doubt the principles themselves.

5   A difficulty is created by the terminology I use in speaking about these different approaches. 'Reparation', according to many people's understanding, can only be made by a wrongdoer. So understood, it is a term wedded to an obligations-centred approach. Indeed, those who take a rights-centred approach tend to prefer terms like 'compensation', 'restoration' or (in Nozick's case) 'rectification'. In order to be true to my semantic decisions (see Introduction), I am forcing the term 'reparative justice' to encompass theories that take either approach. The same goes for the use of the term to encompass reconciliatory approaches – which are regarded by their advocates as being opposed to legalistic approaches that require reparation (associated in this context with restoration).

6   Some philosophers and legal theorists argue that treatment of crime, punishment and reparation in our legal system ought to be changed. For example, Barnett (1977) argues that a system that requires criminals to pay restitution to their victims should replace punishment.

7   Feinberg, 1978, p. 102.

8   Not every one agrees with Feinberg. For example, Zimmerman (1994) argues that the backpacker case is no different from one in which a child or an animal causes damage to property, which does not call for compensation.

9   Swinburne, 1989, p. 74.

10   Ibid., pp. 74–5.

11   Proponents of the second approach include Minow (1998), Shriver (1995) and Tavuchis (1991).

12   Gaus, 1991, pp. 60ff.

13   Aristotle says: 'What the judge aims at doing is to make the parts equal by the penalty he imposes, whereby he takes from the aggressor any gain he may have secured' (1955, p. 148).

14 Gaus, 1991, p. 72.
15 I am here agreeing with Boxill (1972, pp. 119–20).
16 Mulgan stresses this point in his discussion of reconciliation (1998, pp. 187ff).
17 Some people think that there is something intrinsically suspect about 'apologies of state'. How can leaders apologize for everyone in their nation, especially if not everyone is remorseful? How can a leader's apology be taken seriously if he or she is compelled by political circumstances to apologize? These questions can, I think, be answered by pointing out that such apologies are not personal – they are acts of state, and no more require unanimity or the personal endorsement of the leader than any other act of state. However, the question remains whether apology is always going to be the best way of pursuing the objective of reconciliation.
18 Rawls, 1996, p. 134.

Chapter 4 Land Rights and Reparation

1 Lazarus, 1991, p. 81.
2 Goodin, 2000, p. 329.
3 Locke begins with the assumption that a person has 'property in his own person', and thus that his labour belongs to him. 'Whatsoever, then, he removes out of the state that Nature hath provided and left it in, he hath mixed his labour with it, and joined to it something that is his own, and thereby makes it his property' (1978, p. 130).
4 This is argued by Bishop (1977). Kolers (2000) argues, more radically, that the Lockean idea that ownership is conditional on productivity or efficiency is mistaken.
5 After giving serious consideration to Locke's theory of acquisition, Nozick rejects it (1974, pp. 174–5). He supplies no theory of his own, and thus the argument of his book takes the form of a conditional: 'if historical titles can be properly grounded, then . . . '.
6 Waldron (1988, ch. 6) discusses these and other objections to Locke's account of acquisition. For an attempt to defend original acquisition against some of the objections made against it, see Simmons, 1994.
7 Nozick, 1974, pp. 150–4.
8 Ibid., p. 231.
9 Waldron, 1992, p. 28.
10 My colleague Bruce Langtry reminds me that there are occasions on which we believe that 'we were here first' is good justification for possession – for example, when early-bird shoppers are the ones who snap up the bargains. It is more difficult to accept this justification when people are latecomers through no fault of their own, and when what are at stake are their lives and well-being.
11 Locke, 1978, p. 133.

12   If I legitimately appropriate a desert water-hole, and all other water-holes dry up, thus threatening the lives of other desert dwellers, I am no longer entitled to charge what I want for the water (Nozick, 1974, p. 180).
13   Lyons, 1977, p. 370. There are other interpretations of the proviso: for example, that suggested by Simmons (1995, pp. 164–5). Simmons argues that Lockean owners can be forced to downsize their holdings for the sake of the needs of others, but are entitled to retain a 'particularized share'.
14   Lyons, 1977, p. 374.
15   Ibid., p. 375.
16   Walzer, 1977, p. 55.
17   Ibid., p. 55.
18   Waldron, 1992, p. 19.
19   Brown 1970, p. 276.
20   Tully, 1994.
21   The example is from Lea (1998, p. 1), who criticizes Tully for an uncritical acceptance of traditional land rights. Though I think his criticism can be countered, he is right to point out that an appeal to respect for the laws of nations does not answer difficult questions about jurisdiction.
22   Waldron, 1992, p. 6.

Chapter 5   A Matter of Time

1   Booker, 1994, p. v.
2   McNair, 1961, p. 494.
3   I will argue in the second part of this study that individuals can sometimes have reparative entitlements simply as descendants of victims of injustice.
4   Elizabeth made the apology as Queen of New Zealand according to a script prepared by the New Zealand government. For details see Barkan, 2000, p. 264.
5   Sher, 1981, pp. 10–12.
6   Ibid., p. 13.
7   Does this condition exclude too much? My colleague Bruce Langtry offers the following counter-example. 'Suppose Jones spikes your drink with a drug and as a result you crash the car on the way home from the party. Surely Jones is morally responsible for your crash even though he had every reason to believe that your partner would be driving.' Jones's moral responsibility, it seems to me, depends on how much reason Jones had to believe that your partner would be driving – that is, how probable it was that you would be driving instead. What degree of probability we require depends on the likelihood of a very bad effect if our beliefs turn out to be wrong. Maybe we think in this case that the chance of your being the driver was great enough that the risk of giving you

something that would impair your driving shouldn't have been taken. If we do believe this, then the fact that your decision to drive was independent doesn't matter. Once we decide that the person who stabbed A is morally responsible for his death, then the fact that A didn't run away when he had a chance to do so is not an independent action to which his death can reasonably be attributed.

8 Sher, 1981, pp. 16–17.

9 I am making a point similar to that of Sparrow (2000), who argues that the meaning of an injustice depends on the history in which it is embedded.

Chapter 6 All Things Considered

1 There have been two important Australian High Court decisions about native title during the last decade. The first, the Mabo decision in 1992, held that native title was not necessarily extinguished by imposition of Common Law or settlement. The Wik decision of 1996 held that leasehold property could be subject to native title claims.

2 Waldron, 1992, pp. 18–19. Waldron does not say that present possessors have gained the title but his view seems to imply this. A similar justification for reparation is found in Goodin, 1991, pp. 152ff.

3 Waldron does allow that religious ties to particular sites can give a tribe or nation a more persistent claim. See my discussion of this view in ch. 4.

4 A realist is someone who believes that in international politics the best thing for leaders to do, or the course they ought to adopt, is to promote the security or power of their state (or to maintain a balance of power). For two critical discussions of realism see Walzer, 1977, ch. 1, and Cohen, 1984.

5 Leona Lovell, quoted in Read, 1996, p. 69.

6 See Barkan's (2000) discussion of this issue in ch. 8.

7 There are a few philosophers who have combined a concern for equity with a recognition of historical title. For example, Simmons (1995) argues that heirs of the dispossessed may not be entitled to all the possessions of their ancestors. Their title gives them only a right to a 'particularized share' of these possessions – a share compatible with principles of equity. This position requires a defence of historical title (see Simmons, 1994). It also raises the question of whether justice based on title can in all cases be made compatible with justice as equity.

Chapter 7 The Rights of Descendants

1 Feagin and O'Brien, 1999.

2 Boxill, 1972, p. 120.

3 Robinson, 2000, p. 107.

4   See Barkan, 2000, ch. 6.
5   For an account of the controversy in Germany about property in the former GDR, see Dahn, 1998.
6   Some theories of personal identity could be used to question this entitlement. Parfit (1984, pp. 204–17), argues that there is no essence or property of a person that we can use to answer questions about identity through time. Identity is a matter of psychological continuities, and it is not unreasonable to think that old A is not the same person as young A. Since the focus of this study is historical obligations and entitlements, I will not discuss the problems raised for reparative justice by this theory. Nevertheless, I think that the position I present in chapter 8, suitably elaborated, could be used to argue that even if old A is not the same as young A, old A may be able to claim some of what was wrongly taken from young A.
7   For a defence of the idea that group membership can be a basis for compensation, see Fishkin, 1991.
8   Sher, 1979. He has in mind cases where the injustice was done not long before an individual was conceived. It seems plausible to compare the well-being of this individual with the child that would have been born to these parents in a world in which the injustice had not been done. In a more recent, unpublished paper, 'Transgenerational compensation,' he argues that those born after the injustice took place are themselves injured by a failure to rectify the wrong.
9   Bittker, 1973, ch. 1.
10 Kershnar (1999) makes this point.
11 Locke, 1978, p. 148.
12 This is part of an argument against inheritance presented by Haslett (1986, pp. 145–8). He also suggests that the desire to provide for retirement is probably a stronger motivation for saving in modern Western societies than the desire to provide an inheritance for children.
13 Levy, 1983, pp. 547–50.
14 Rawls, 1971, pp. 103ff.
15 Waldron, 1992, pp. 8–9.
16 Ibid., p. 10.

Chapter 8   Inheritance, Equity and Reparation

1   Levy, 1983, p. 545.
2   Lomasky, 1987, p. 270.
3   Ibid., p. 213.
4   See Callahan, 1987. Nevertheless, the idea that the dead can be harmed has been strongly defended by some philosophers, especially Pitcher (1984).
5   Aristotle, 1980, bk I, ch. 11, p. 23.

6 Partridge claims that theories of the self show that 'well functioning human beings identify with, and seek to further, the well-being, preservation and endurance of communities, locations, causes, artifacts, institutions, ideals, and so on, that are outside themselves and that they hope will flourish beyond their own lifetimes' (1980, p. 204).

7 Feinberg, 1974, p. 58.

8 Haslett, 1986, pp. 123–6.

9 Ibid., p. 137.

10 Simmons (1995, p. 162) defends the same position, but for different reasons.

11 Rawls, 1971, p. 128.

12 In this respect Rawls is following in the footsteps of the traditional social contract theorists, like Locke and Hobbes, who also supposed that the makers of the social contract represent members of their families and other dependents.

13 Rawls, 1971, pp. 284ff.

14 See Rawls's discussion of moral development (1971, pp. 462–7).

15 Waldron (1992, pp. 19–20), makes a similar point about the survival of entitlements in some cases.

Chapter 9   Reparation and Injustices to Family Lines

1 Robinson, 2000, p. 216.

2 Ibid.

3 This information comes from the report of the Human Rights and Equal Opportunity Commission (1997). Since the publication of the report, there have been debates about how many children were affected and how coercive the policy was. Nevertheless, the above information seems to be accurate.

4 As late as 1858, the papal police, with the encouragement of Pope Pius IX, kidnapped a six-year-old Jewish child and placed him in an institution where he was educated in the Catholic faith. The efforts of his parents to get him back were frustrated by the Pope, who officially adopted him. The abduction was justified on the ground that the child had been secretly baptized by a Christian servant (Cornwell, 1999, p. 11).

5 This statement of the rights of Jewish parents is found in a medieval German law book dating from c.1503. Kisch attributes the view it expresses to St Jerome (1970, p. 59).

6 Kymlicka, 1989, pp. 162ff.

7 Since in A Theory of Justice (1971) Rawls assumes strict compliance with principles of justice, he is not concerned with how representatives of family lines would respond to the possibility of injustice. Nevertheless, it seems reasonable to consider how people with this perspective would respond in a less than ideal situation.

8   Human Rights and Equal Opportunity Commission, 1997, pp. 282ff.
9   Robinson, 2000, p. 107. Some of the people interviewed by Paris thought that there ought to be a national monument commemorating the lives and deaths of slaves (2001, p. 232).
10 Quote from the Black Manifesto in Bittker, 1973, p. 8.
11 See Browne, 1993.
12 This is what Robinson is really demanding (2000, p. 173); and Boxill's closing remarks can be similarly interpreted (1972, p. 122).
13 This point has often been made against reverse or positive discrimination programmes – for example, by Rossum (1980, p. 160).

Conclusion: Justice and Transgenerational Relationships

1   Quoted in Bredvold and Ross, 1961, pp. 43–4.
2   Laslett, 1992, p. 24. Laslett attributes the concern of philosophers regarding future generations to the rise of the environmental movement.
3   For some discussions of the problems, see Barry and Sikora 1978; Partridge 1980; Laslett and Fishkin, 1992.
4   Parfit, 1984, sections 130–1.
5   Laslett, 1992, pp. 25ff.
6   Rawls, 1971, p. 289.
7   For example, Michael Sandel (1982) criticizes Rawls for assuming that individuals have no essential social relations.
8   Baier argues that we would do our predecessors, as well as future generations, an injustice if we fail to maintain the institutions that they laboured to provide for posterity (1980, p. 180).

References

Anaya, S. J. 1996: *Indigenous Peoples in International Law.* Oxford / New York: Oxford University Press.

Aristotle 1955: *The Ethics*, tr. J. A. K. Thomson. Harmondsworth: Penguin.

Aristotle 1980: *Nichomachean Ethics*, tr. D. Ross. Oxford / New York: Oxford University Press.

Baier, A. 1980: The rights of past and future persons. In Partridge, 1980, pp. 171–86.

Barkan, E. 2000: *Guilt of Nations: Restitution and Negotiating Historic Injustice.* New York / London: W. W. Norton & Co.

Barnett, R. E. 1977: Restitution: a new paradigm of criminal justice. *Ethics*, 87, 279–301.

Barry, B. 1978: Circumstances of justice and future generations. In Barry and Sikora, 1978, pp. 204–48.

Barry B. and Sikora R. I. (eds) 1978: *Obligations to Future Generations*, Philadelphia: Temple University Press.

Bedau, H. 1972: Compensatory justice and the Black Manifesto. *Monist*, 56, 20–42.

Bigelow, J., Pargetter, R. and Young, R. 1990: Land, well-being and compensation. *Australasian Journal of Philosophy*, 68, 330–46.

Bishop, J. D. 1977: Locke's theory of original appropriation and the right of settlement in Iroquois territory. *Canadian Journal of Philosophy*, 27, 311–38.

Bittker, B. 1973: *The Case for Black Reparations.* New York: Random House.

Blackstone, W. (ed.) 1974: *Philosophy and Environmental Crisis.* Athens, Ga.: University of Georgia Press.

Booker, M. 1994: *Conflict in the Balkans.* Sydney: Catalyst Press.

Bourrie, M. 1998: Canada apologizes for abuse of native peoples. *IPS News*, 8 Jan.: oneworld.org / ips2 / Jan98 / canada2.html.

Boxill, B. 1972: Morality of reparation. *Social Theory and Practice*, 2, 113–23.

Bredvold, L. I. and Ross R. G. (eds) 1961: *The Philosophy of Edmund Burke*. Ann Arbor: University of Michigan Press.

Brooks, R. L. 1999a: The age of apology. In R. L. Brooks (ed.), *When Sorry Isn't Enough: The Controversy over Apology and Reparation for Human Injustice*, New York: New York University Press, 3–11.

Brooks, R. L. 1999b: Not even an apology? In R. L. Brooks (ed.), *When Sorry Isn't Enough: The Controversy over Apology and Reparation for Human Injustice*, New York: New York University Press, 309–54.

Brown, D. 1970: *Bury My Heart at Wounded Knee: An Indian History of the American West*. New York/Chicago: Holt, Rinehart & Winston.

Browne, R. S. 1991: Let's talk about reparations for slavery. *New York Times*, 7 Jan., A16.

Browne, R. S. 1993: The economic basis for reparations to black Americans. *Review of Black Political Economy*, 21, 99–110.

Brownlie, I. (ed.) 1995: Vienna convention on the law of treaties. In *Basic Documents in International Law*, 4th edn, Oxford: Oxford University Press, 388–425.

Callahan, J. C. 1987: On harming the dead. *Ethics*, 97, 341–52.

Chapman, J. W. (ed.) 1991: *Nomos*, vol. 33: *Compensatory Justice*. New York: New York University Press.

Cohen, M. 1984: Moral skepticism and international relations. *Philosophy and Public Affairs*, 13, 299–346.

Cornwell, John 1999: *Hitler's Pope: The Secret History of Pius XII*. Harmondsworth: Penguin.

Costo, R. and Henry, J. 1977: *Indian Treaties: Two Centuries of Dishonor*. San Francisco: Indian Historical Press.

Cowan, T. 1997: Discounting and restitution. In *Philosophy and Public Affairs*, 26, 168–85.

Dahn, D. 1998: *Wir bleiben hier oder wem gehört der Osten: Vom Kampf um Häuser und Wohnungen in den neuen Bundesländern*. Hamburg: Rowholt.

Desmond, E. 1995: Japan: finally a real apology, *Time*, New York, 149 (2), 28 Aug., 47.

Feagin, J. R. and O'Brien, E. 1999: The long-overdue reparations for African Americans. In R. L. Brooks (ed.), *When Sorry Isn't Enough: The Controversy over Apology and Reparation for Human Injustice*, New York: New York University Press, 419–20.

Feinberg, J. 1968: Collective responsibility. *Journal of Philosophy*, 65, 674–88.

Feinberg, J. 1974: The rights of animals and unborn generations. In Blackstone, 1974, pp. 43–68.

Feinberg, J. 1978: Voluntary euthanasia and the inalienable right to life. *Philosophy and Public Affairs*, 7, 93–123.

Fishkin, J. S. 1991: Justice between generations: compensation, identity, and group membership. In Chapman 1991, pp. 85–96.

French, L. A. 1994: *The Winds of Injustice: American Indians and the U.S. Government*. New York / London: Garland Publishing.

Gaus, G. F. 1991: Does compensation restore equality? In Chapman, 1991, pp. 45–81.

Gilbert, M. 1996: On feeling guilt for what one's group has done. In M. Gilbert, *Living Together: Rationality, Sociality, and Obligation*, Lanham, Md.: Rowman & Littlefield, 375–90.

Goff, Lord and Jones, G. 1993: *The Law of Restitution*. London: Sweet & Maxwell.

Goodin, R. E. 1991: Compensation and redistribution. In Chapman, 1991, pp. 143–69.

Goodin, R. E. 2000: Waitangi tales. In *Australasian Journal of Philosophy*, 78, 309–33.

Hare, R. M. 1963: *Freedom and Reason*. Oxford: Oxford University Press.

Haslett, D. W. 1986: Is inheritance justified? *Philosophy and Public Affairs*, 15, 122–55.

Human Rights and Equal Opportunity Commission 1997: *Bringing them Home: Report of the National Inquiry into the Separation of Aboriginal and Torres Strait Islander Children from their Families*. Sydney: Human Rights and Equal Opportunity Commission.

Jedlicki, J. 1990: Heritage and collective responsibility. In I. Maclean et al., 1990, pp. 53–76.

Kershnar, S. 1999: Are the descendants of slaves owed compensation for slavery? *Journal of Applied Philosophy*, 16, 95–101.

Kirgis, F. L. 1997: International agreements and U.S. law. In *ASIL Insight*: asil.org / insights / insigh10.htm.

Kisch, G. 1970: *The Jews in Medieval Germany: A Study of their Legal and Social Status*, 2nd edn. New York: KTAV Press.

Kolers, A. 2000: The Lockean efficiency argument and aboriginal land rights. *Australasian Journal of Philosophy*, 78, 391–405.

Kymlicka, W. 1989: *Liberalism, Community, and Culture*. New York: Oxford University Press.

Kymlicka, W. 1995: *Multicultural Citizenship*. Oxford: Clarendon Press.

Lamont, W. D. 1941: Justice: distributive and corrective. *Philosophy*, 16 (1), 3–18.

Laslett, P. 1992: Is there a generational contract? In Laslett and Fishkin, 1992, pp. 24–47.

Laslett, P. and J. S. Fishkin (eds), 1992: *Justice between Age Groups and Generations*. New Haven, Conn.: Yale University Press.

Lazarus, E. 1991: *Black Hills, White Justice: The Sioux Nation versus the United States, 1775 to the Present*. New York: Harper Collins.

Lea, D. R. 1998: Aboriginal entitlement and conservative theory. *Journal of Applied Philosophy*, 15, 1–14.

Levy, M. B. 1983: Liberal equality and inherited wealth. *Political Theory*, 11, 545–64.

Litan, R. E. 1977: On rectification in Nozick's minimal state. *Political Theory*, 5, 233–45.

Locke, J. 1978: *Two Treatises of Government*. London/Melbourne: Dent.

Lomasky, L. 1987: *Persons, Rights and the Moral Community*. Oxford/New York: Oxford University Press.

Lyons, D. 1977: The new Indian land claims and the original right to land. *Social Theory and Practice*, 4, 249–72.

MacIntyre, A. 1981: *After Virtue: A Study in Moral Theory*, 2nd edn. London: Duckworth.

Maclean, I., Montefiore, A, and Winch, P. (eds) 1990: *The Political Responsibility of Intellectuals*. Cambridge/New York: Cambridge University Press.

Magee, R. V. 1993: The master's tools, from the bottom up: responses to African-American reparations theory in mainstream and outsider remedies discourse. *Virginia Law Review*, 79, 863–916.

McNair, A. (Lord) 1961: *Law of Treaties*. Oxford: Clarendon Press.

Minow, M. 1998: *Between Vengeance and Forgiveness: Facing History after Genocide and Mass Violence*. Boston: Beacon Press.

Mulgan, R. 1998: Citizenship and legitimacy in post-colonial Australia. In Peterson and Sanders, 1998, pp. 179–95.

Nozick, R. 1974: *Anarchy, State, and Utopia*. New York: Basic Books.

Orange, C. 1987: *The Treaty of Waitangi*. Wellington, NZ/Sydney: Allen and Unwin.

Parfit, D. 1984: *Reasons and Persons*. Oxford: Clarendon Press.

Paris, E. 2001: *Long Shadows: Truth, Lies and History*. New York/London: Bloomsbury.

Partridge, E. 1980: Why care about the future? In Partridge 1980: 203–20.

Partridge, E. (ed.) 1980, *Responsibilities to Future Generations*, Buffalo, NY: Prometheus Books.

Peterson, N. and Sanders, W. (eds) 1998: *Citizenship and Indigenous Australians: Changing Conceptions and Possibilities*. Cambridge: Cambridge University Press.

Pitcher, G. 1984: Misfortunes of the dead. *American Philosophical Quarterly*, 21, 183–8.

Rao, P. S. S. Rama 1981: The theory of compensatory justice: a case for the third world. *Philosophy and Social Action*, 7, 5–18.

Rawls, J. 1972: *A Theory of Justice*. Cambridge, Mass.: Harvard University Press.

Rawls, J. 1996: *Political Liberalism*. New York: Columbia University Press.

Read, P. 1996: *Returning to Nothing: The Meaning of Lost Places*. Cambridge/New York: Cambridge University Press.

Robinson, R. 2000: *The Debt: What America Owes to Blacks*. New York, Harmondsworth: Penguin.

Rossum, R. A. 1980: *Discrimination and the Constitutional Debate*. New York/Basel: Marcel Dekker.

Sandel, M. (1982): *Liberalism and the Limits of Justice*. Cambridge: Cambridge University Press.

Scheffler, S. 1997: Relationships and responsibilities. *Philosophy and Public Affairs*, 26, 189–209.

Sharp, A. 1999: *Justice and the Maori: Maori Claims in New Zealand Political Arguments*, 2nd edn. Oxford / Auckland, NZ: Oxford University Press.

Sher, G. 1979: Compensation and transworld personal identity. *Monist*, 62, 378–91.

Sher, G. 1981: Ancient wrongs and modern rights. *Philosophy and Public Affairs*, 10, 3–17.

Shriver, D. W. Jr. 1995: *An Ethic for Enemies: Forgiveness in Politics*. Oxford / New York: Oxford University Press.

Simmons, A. J. 1994: Original-acquisition justifications of private property. *Social Philosophy and Policy*, 11, 63–84.

Simmons, A. J. 1995: Historical rights and fair shares. *Law and Philosophy*, 14, 149–84.

Simmons, A. J. 1996: Associative political obligations. *Ethics*, 106, 247–73.

Sparrow, R. 2000: History and collective responsibility. *Australasian Journal of Philosophy*, 78, 346–73.

Stanley, A. 2000: Pope asks forgiveness for errors of the church over 2,000 years. *New York Times on the Web*, 13 Mar.: nytimes.com / library / world / global / 031300pope-apologize.html.

Swinburne, R. 1989: *Responsibility and Atonement*. Oxford: Clarendon Press.

Tavuchis, N. 1991: *Mea Culpa: A Sociology of Apology and Reconciliation*. Stanford, Calif.: Stanford University Press.

Tully, J. 1994: Aboriginal property and western theory: recovering a middle ground. *Social Philosophy and Policy*, 11, 153–80.

Waldron, J. 1988: *The Right to Private Property*. Oxford / New York: Oxford University Press.

Waldron, J. 1992: Superseding historical injustice. *Ethics*, 103, 4–28.

Walzer, M. 1977: *Just and Unjust Wars: A Moral Argument with Historical Illustrations*. Harmondsworth: Penguin.

Wheeler, S. C. III 1997: Reparations reconstructed. *American Philosophical Quarterly*, 34, 301–18.

Zimmerman, M. J. 1994: Rights, compensation, and culpability. *Law and Philosophy*, 13, 419–50.

Index